DISCARD

*f*P

Also by David W. Shaw

Inland Passage
Daring the Sea
Flying Cloud

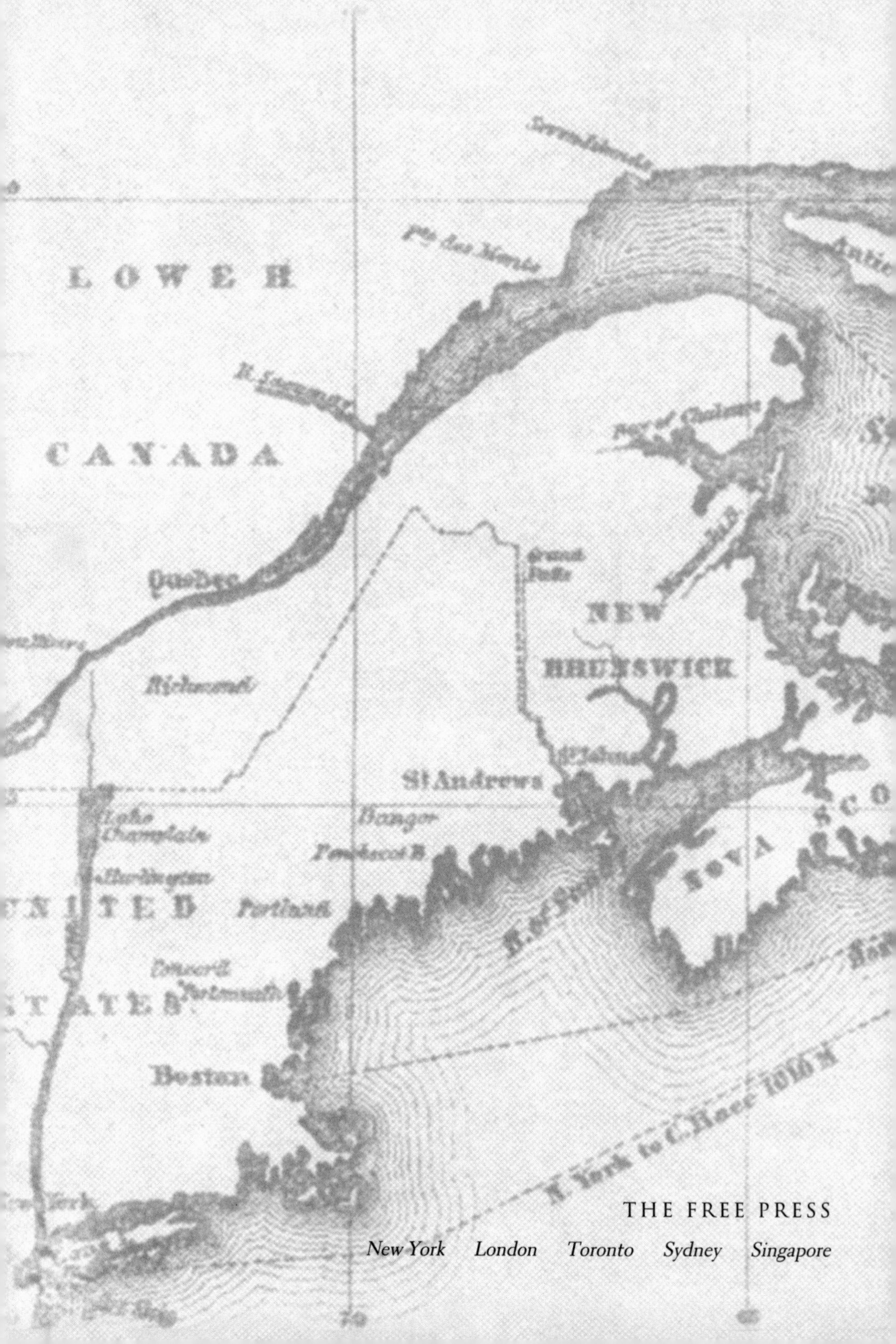

THE FREE PRESS
New York London Toronto Sydney Singapore

THE SEA SHALL EMBRACE THEM

THE TRAGIC STORY OF THE STEAMSHIP ARCTIC

DAVID W. SHAW

THE FREE PRESS
A Division of Simon & Schuster, Inc.
1230 Avenue of the Americas
New York, NY 10020

THE FREE PRESS and colophon are trademarks
of Simon & Schuster, Inc.

For information about special discounts for bulk purchases,
please contact Simon & Schuster Special Sales:
1-800-456-6798 or business@simonandschuster.com

Designed by Lisa Chovnick
Illustrations in text by Margaret Westergaard

All images in the picture section are reproduced by courtesy of
the Mariners' Museum, Newport News, Virginia.

Manufactured in the United States of America

1   3   5   7   9   10   8   6   4   2

Library of Congress Cataloging-in-Publication Data

Shaw, David W.
The sea shall embrace them : the tragic story of the steamship
Arctic / David W. Shaw.
p.   cm.
Includes bibliographical references (p.   ).
1. Arctic (Steamship).   2. Shipwrecks—North Atlantic Ocean.   I. Title.

G530.A67 S52   2002
910'.916344—dc21   2001040956

ISBN 0-7432-2217-2 (alk. paper)

For all those
whom the sea has claimed.
May they rest in peace
in its embrace.

For they have heard evil tidings . . . there is sorrow on the sea;

it cannot be quiet.

—Jeremiah 49.23

CONTENTS

Contents

PREFACE

THE TRAGIC LOSS OF STEAMSHIP *Arctic* on September 27, 1854, represents one of the most important chapters in American maritime history. This book attempts to tell *Arctic*'s story as a complete narrative for the first time. The level of detail in these pages will surprise many readers. What made such detail possible was, simply, a multitude of contemporary documents.

Although I could not interview survivors as some authors of nonfiction accounts of more recent maritime disasters have been able to do, constructing a lively, rigorously authentic tale without author interviews is not unprecedented. And in this case, abundant testimony exists from eyewitnesses who survived the shipwreck and reported what they saw to newspapers such as the *New York Herald* and the *New York Daily Times*. This was a disaster that made headlines almost every day for a month. A close study and comparison of the numerous accounts revealed the drama I have set out here. Indeed, so vivid was some of the testimony that I confess it haunted me for several months during the writing of this manuscript.

On a few occasions I have suggested a person was feeling one thing or another that cannot be absolutely proven, but I stand by these suggestions as insights gained inductively through my reading of the volumes of contemporary testimony.

My efforts to provide an accurate telling of this story are more fully explained in a further note at the end of the book. Suffice it to say here that this is so rich a tale because of the observations preserved in the public record. My thanks to the diligence of the reporters who uncovered the truth as best they could in the weeks following the disaster.

SEPTEMBER 28, 1854

VEILS OF FOG swirled around the bow of the Canadian bark *Huron*. The gray mist closed in on the headsails, rendering them almost invisible from the poop deck. Bound for Quebec, *Huron* made her way under full sail toward Cabot Strait, a wide swath of current-ripped water between the islands of Cape Breton and Newfoundland, gateway to the Gulf of St. Lawrence and the funnel of the vast St. Lawrence River estuary. She seemed to cut a path into oblivion, alone on an empty sea. The comforting warmth of fires burning in the kitchen stoves of the simple dwellings ashore was as distant as the wan sun hidden behind an overcast sky darkening with the approach of dusk. The day was much like any other in late September on the Grand Banks fishing grounds—cold and damp with a mounting swell rolling in from the North Atlantic that foretold the arrival of yet another bout of stormy weather.

The lookouts stationed on the forecastle deck took turns blowing the little air horn. Each man spelled the other when his mate became winded, which did not take long. The shrill blasts of the horn, a trumpet-like device, could not reach the ears of crews aboard other ships unless they sailed near enough to pose an imminent threat of collision. But Captain Wall was a conscientious man, and with the owner's son, Wellington Cameron, aboard *Huron*, it was wise to adhere to the unwritten laws of the sea no matter how ludicrous it appeared to the sailors under his command. The faint bleats of the horn continued.

The fog, as it always did when the wind blew fresh, tore into patches, some thick and impenetrable, others with translucence that allowed visibility to improve up to a half-mile or more. Mindful of their duty, the lookouts took advantage of the breaks to redouble their vigilance, not wanting to miss an opportunity to spy danger. The Grand Banks represented an intersection of the coastal and transatlantic shipping lanes, and scores of fishing schooners peppered the sea. Even in late September, the summer fishing season at an end, the place was busier than most stretches of ocean. As the curtains closed in again, one of the lookouts straightened his back and quickly lifted his spyglass. Out of the gloom emerged a shape, slowly at first as the ship sailed on. It looked like a dory, perhaps one separated from the mother ship, her crew of fishermen wondering about the fate of their missing friends. However, it soon became apparent to the lookouts that the little craft was a lifeboat filled with men.

"Lifeboat fine on the starboard bow!" the lookout cried.

"Lifeboat to starboard, aye," the officer on deck responded.

Aft on the poop deck, Captain Wall raised his spyglass and squinted into the deepening darkness. Sure enough, the lookout's observation proved correct. It was indeed a lifeboat, and dangerously overloaded. The men in it paddled toward them with makeshift oars made of planks and axes. Some dug their hands into the frigid water to help propel the boat. It struck Wall as peculiar that the lifeboat lacked even one set of proper oars.

Wall turned to his first officer and ordered him to bring the vessel round, head almost to the wind. The helmsman turned the wheel slowly while the crew scurried on deck to man the braces and other lines needed to control the sails. Canvas shook and thundered in the breeze. Blocks banged on deck and in the rigging as the main topsail backed and fell still, the wind pressing it against the mainmast and shrouds. The ship's other sails still drew forcing the bark to a stop.

The lifeboat was soon alongside, and Wall's crew helped the men stumble aboard. Weak and exhausted from their ordeal, many fell to the deck unable to walk or even stand. Two of the castaways refused to leave the boat. Their voices hoarse and ragged, they begged Wall to send a crew with oars and thole pins (oarlocks) into the boat, saying there was another survivor on a raft a short distance away.

A few minutes later, the lone man on the nearby raft, Peter Mc-Cabe, heard the splash of oars and the voices of the men in the boat. Inches from him, the white faces of corpses trapped beneath the raft, their bodies "much gnawed by fishes" and made buoyant from the life preservers, peered up at him from the spaces between the loosely lashed spars.

McCabe described his moment of salvation in the October 12 edition of the *New York Herald*:

> I was alone on the raft, not a solitary being was alive out of [more than] seventy; but still my hopes continued strong. The night of the second day was about closing on me, and during the whole time I had been in the water I had not eaten a particle of anything or drank a drop. My strength I found was beginning to give way, and my sight had become so dim that I could not perceive objects a few feet off, even the ghastly faces of the dead, that looked up at me from under the raft, were hardly discernible.
>
> I determined at making one more effort for life. I raised myself upon my knees upon the raft, and through the dusk of the evening I saw, or thought I saw, a vessel. My strength seemed to revive, and in a few minutes I heard the voices of persons in a boat approaching me. Ten minutes later, I too would have gone, but Providence had mercy on me, and after twenty-six hours of exposure I was by its mercy preserved from a watery grave.

When all the men came back aboard, Captain Wall, his officers, and Wellington Cameron learned the tragic details concerning the loss of the steamship *Arctic* with more than three hundred souls aboard. She was one of the largest and most luxurious passenger vessels in the world, the pride of the Collins Line out of New York, bound for that port from Liverpool. Plucked from the sea were Francis Dorian, third officer, twenty-six crewmen, including Peter McCabe, and five male passengers.

Dusk faded into night. *Huron* got under way with a raw southeasterly wind off her port quarter filling the sails wet with condensation. Water dripped from rigging and pattered on deck. The bow lifted and fell to the swells. Forward, on the forecastle deck, the lookouts blew the foghorn, its mournful wail dull and faint as it echoed over the waves through the heavy, moisture-laden atmosphere. At Wall's orders, other crewmen fired rockets in hope of attracting the attention of any other victims who might be clinging to wreckage in the ship's path. The fuses were lit. A hiss and a whoosh, followed with the thud of a muffled explosion, punctuated the intermittent silences between blasts of the foghorn. White halos appeared in the blackness and vanished, the sparks twinkling out one by one.

Standing on the windward side of the poop deck, alone and troubled, Captain Wall considered the events of the day. Shipwrecks were common enough in the waters of the North Atlantic and down the coast of the United States all the way to the Gulf of Mexico. Every year, approximately ninety American oceangoing sailing ships sank in the dangerous waters of the Bahamas, Cape Hatteras, Nantucket Shoals, Cape Cod, Cape Sable, and Cape Race. Additional American coastal traders went down or were stranded on the beaches and rocky ledges.

The sea took European vessels as well. Just a few weeks past, cruising in dense fog, the brand new Inman Line steamship *City of Philadelphia* valued at $600,000 ran hard aground on the rocks off Newfoundland's Cape Race. The wreck counted as one of many losses to British shipping that occurred in 1854. However, no one perished when she struck, unlike what had happened to *Arctic*. That unfortunate conclusion became clear to Wall and the others aboard *Huron*

4

after they listened to the stories of the rescued men. Yet some of the sailors seemed guarded in their testimony, as if they were selective in the details they related, and Wall did not understand why.

Snugging his heavy pea coat close, Wall followed the stripe of the latest rocket as it cut through the darkness and exploded with a distant boom. Questions nagged at him, deeply upsetting and persistent. A chill went through him, causing him to pull his coat even tighter to his chest. He felt the kind of cold touch that no amount of clothing could repel, a hint of unease he could not quite place but which was real enough. Like the flit of a bat's wing on a dark night, a shadow against the stars, it danced away before he could see the shape of its evil meaning.

CHAPTER ONE

GENTLEMANLY DEMEANOR

L OW SCUD FILLED THE SKY in the pale light of a late spring afternoon in 1849 as a fierce westerly gale ripped the tops off the waves
of the North Atlantic one thousand miles from the nearest land. Spray
blew eastward toward Europe on the heels of the wind. It flew through
the air onto the backs of the breakers and formed thick layers of foam
that ran in streaks across the black surface of the water before the force
of the storm toppled the waves into the troughs twenty to thirty feet
below. The howl of the wind and the rumble of the sea drowned out
the curses of the sailors shivering at their sail stations on the deck of
the Red Star packet *Constellation*. The men stood ready for yet one
more struggle in a cycle of brute will and brawn required to sail the big
square-rigged ship home against the prevailing gales of winter.

Aft on the poop deck, Captain James C. Luce scanned the ocean
with the practiced eye of a seasoned mariner familiar with the hazards
of the transatlantic trade. He was a tall, strongly built man with a rakish mustache, which made him look more like a cavalry officer accustomed to the pleasures of the drawing room than a typical Yankee
captain with a bushy full beard and weather-beaten skin. Luce
watched the seas, searching for a smooth stretch between sets of the
larger waves roaring toward his vessel off the right side of the bow.
Fishermen around the port of New York, his destination, called such
smooths a *slatch*. It was a word for the order within the chaos that always existed, but it had to be discerned. The timing of his next move,

turning the ship's stern through the eye of the wind, was crucial in such severe conditions. Luce was a patient captain fully aware of the danger a lapse of judgment might mean to his ship, the crew, and the hundreds of Irish, German, and French immigrants locked below in the packet's stinking hold. He intended to make no rash decisions.

Luce found the right moment for action. He shouted orders to his first officer, who moved forward along the lifelines strung fore and aft on the weather deck and signaled the second mate at his post near the foremast. The packet eased off the wind, bringing it from hard on the bow back toward the stern as the ship turned. At the same time, the sailors adjusted the yards supporting the straining sails bellied out under the press of the storm. When the wind blew directly behind the ship, the sails on the mainmast formed a lee, a protective wall that decreased the strength of the gale on the sails forward. The crew quickly turned the yards for the new tack, pivoting them on the mast with considerable difficulty. As the sails filled, the foremast bent and appeared ready to crash to the deck. But the ship kept turning, and soon she was safely on a port tack. The wind now screamed hard on the left side of the bow.

Throughout the preceding five days, all hands had been on deck most of the time, under the watchful stares of Captain Luce and his officers. The Yankee captain drove on in a gale no British master would consider fighting, true to the tradition of the New York packets. Every stitch of canvas that *Constellation* could set was up, reduced in size through a process known as reefing, but up and drawing just the same. The ship labored hard as she sailed a zigzag course against the wind. Solid water weighing tons swept the deck. It drowned some of the chickens, pigs, and sheep in their pens near the deckhouse and carried away anything not lashed down tight. It threatened to pitch unwary crewmen overboard to certain death.

The immigrants below had eaten no hot food for days because of the storm, and while Luce felt compassion for them, their hardship amounted to nothing more than the way of life at sea when sailing on a schedule. The entire ship's company suffered from exhaustion, hunger, and the cold. Ice coated the rigging and decks, adding to the danger and misery of this voyage, *Constellation*'s first of three for 1849, taking her from New York to Liverpool and back on a regular schedule regardless of the season, the weather, and the amount of freight, human or otherwise, lodged in the hold.

A packet sailed when the schedule promised and reached port as close to the advertised arrival date as possible. It was up to the captain to ensure she did not falter on the way for any reason. Not every ship was called a packet. Only those that kept a schedule enjoyed that burgeoning distinction of the steam era. Ships that sailed when the weather was fair and holds filled with cargo were called regular traders, and they were far less profitable for both their owners and the masters who commanded them.

It had been so ever since the Black Ball Line of sailing ships went into service in 1818 and became the first packet line in the United States, when Luce was just a boy of thirteen. Sailing on a schedule back then represented something new and innovative, and uniquely American. Most shipowners and captains preferred good weather and full holds prior to embarking on ocean voyages, and they did not depart until the requisite conditions prevailed. Delays for merchants waiting for their commodities and delays for passengers waiting to reach their destinations were considered part of doing business. Ships seldom sailed in winter because of the risk of potential disaster, reducing the trading season and diminishing profits. These traditional practices struck Yankee traders as timid and inefficient.

Thus, the founders of the Black Ball Line took the initiative. They established regular sailing schedules and stuck to them even if it meant losing money in the short term. To set their ships apart from the regular traders, every vessel in the line sported an enormous black cannonball painted on the fore topsail. The distinctive markings presented quite a sight as a Black Baller hove into view over the horizon. The Black Ball Line quickly prospered, and other wealthy men, mostly from New York, followed the company's example and started lines of their own. The Red Star and Swallowtail lines began operating in 1822. Business boomed as Great Britain and the United States started trading again after the War of 1812, engaging in a bloodless rivalry that remained intense. In 1825, there were thirty-two American oceangoing packets. That number had jumped to fifty-two during Luce's nearly three decades at sea.

Since those early days of the packet service, with its promise of departures on a specific day and hour, the U.S. merchant marine had shown the rest of the world what it meant to sail fast and well. The packets of the Black Ball, Red Star, Swallowtail, Dramatic, and New Line were the pride of the nation, besting the British for three decades. These Yankee ships crossed the Atlantic from New York on an average of eighteen to twenty-eight days, covering the 3,137 nautical miles between that port and Liverpool at a speed of six to eight knots, and sometimes swifter than that. In 1847, the packet *Isaac Wright* made the eastbound passage to Liverpool in just thirteen days, the equivalent speed of a steamship. However, the westbound passages against the prevailing winds took an average of thirty-three days. The steamers always did better than that, even the plodders.

But the supremacy of the American merchant marine had been fading since the inauguration in 1840 of the steamships of the British-backed Samuel Cunard. Heavily subsidized with funds from the British Admiralty, Cunard's steamers were the first to offer efficient, reliable service between the Old and New Worlds. As regular as clockwork, Cunard liners traveled from Liverpool to Halifax, Nova Scotia, then on to Boston before heading back to England. An average crossing took about thirteen days. Cunard expanded his line to offer service direct from Liverpool to New York in 1848, and the British annual subsidy increased to £145,000 sterling to help finance the operation of a fleet of ten oceangoing steamships. American attempts to establish a similarly efficient, reliable line of steamships failed throughout the 1840s, much to the great embarrassment of the American public and, in particular, Congress. The failures resulted in part because Congress was slow to provide the money needed to compete against the British.

Speaking of the Cunard liners in Congress in the early 1840s, Senator James Asheton Bayard said, "America will soon become tired of being informed now of British maritime supremacy. I suggest cost must not be considered [in establishing U.S. steamship lines subsidized by the government]. I suggest, too, that Congress grant a carefully selected American shipping expert a completely free hand to proceed with the absolute conquest of this man Cunard." Support for such an enterprise increased, and in 1845 Congress agreed to subsidize American steamship companies. The initial results were far from satisfactory.

Prior to the emergence of the transatlantic steamship, which began in earnest in the late 1830s due to British backing of the new technology, Luce had witnessed the rise of American packets. He had prospered from his service in the most elite branch of the merchant marine, only to see his fortunes on the ebb in the few years preceding his voyage on *Constellation* in 1849. The packets lost the contracts to carry mail between Europe and the United States, and the merchants shifted the fine freight and shipments of gold and silver coins to the Cunard line of steamships. The first-class passengers who once filled the cabins on the westbound passages had decreased from hundreds to a mere handful, though many still chose the New York packets for the eastbound crossings. These wise travelers rightfully thought the luxury accommodations available on the best of the New York sailing packets outdid the spartan cabins and awful food of a Cunard steamer, which were often called "smoke boxes." A swift packet headed east before the prevailing westerlies sailed nearly as fast as a Cunarder. Comfort won out over speed in these cases.

Writing in the mid-1870s in his four-volume collection, *History of Merchant Shipping and Ancient Commerce*, British merchant W. S. Lindsay described the good management and prosperity of the Yankee packet captain:

Thus young men of good position and talent were led to enter the American merchant service, and had much greater inducements than they would then have had in Great Britain to take a zealous interest in the economy, discipline, and success of the ship they commanded; and this, not merely from the fact that they were well recommended, but from the confidential and courteous treatment they received from their employers. Captains of the larger class of packets or merchant-ships, therefore, could not only afford to live as gentlemen, but, if men of good character and fair manners (which they generally were), they were received into the best mercantile circles on shore. They were also allowed, besides their fixed salary, a percentage (usually 2.5 percent) on all freights, and by various other privileges (particularly in relation to passengers [who routinely gave their favored captains large bonuses]), they were thus enabled to save money and to become, in time, merchants and shipowners on their own account, a custom which prevailed, to a large extent, in the New England States.

At its height in the mid-1830s, prior to the early emergence of the transatlantic steamship, captains such as Luce earned annual salaries of approximately $3,000 per year, the equivalent of $54,000 in U.S. currency today. Added to this fixed income was a master's fee from the mails, amounting to $1,500 per year, plus his percentage on the freight and any "gifts" from the passengers. The captain often owned an interest in his vessel, which added further to his net worth. The life was hard, but it was rewarding. It still was, at least for the upper crust of the masters serving aboard the packets.

As the 1840s drew near to a close, Luce now saw the plum position of the Yankee packet captain threatened by economic pressures from England and, more specifically, from the ships of Samuel Cunard. Standing on the deck of *Constellation* in a storm in early 1849, he was smart enough to see that the future did not appear economically bright for the packets. The presence of poor immigrants aboard evidenced this. The owners of New York packets once shunned the immigrant trade, leaving it to the regular traders. They now solicited it with cheap fares at $20 a head just to ensure a profit for the return trip home. Profits from the immigrants went directly to shipowners; the master received nothing extra for the trouble of tending his human freight. On the regular traders, it stank below deck. Even on *Constellation*, with a compassionate, diligent, and civil captain, conditions were poor.

Captain Luce satisfied himself that all was in order on deck. He peered through the gale's scudding spray to check the trim of the sails. Two men at the wheel struggled to keep the ship on course. Luce sent half the crew off watch below. He left the poop deck in the charge of his first officer and went below himself, retiring to the confines of his private cabin, where he stripped off his oilskins and the wet clothes beneath them and changed into his last dry wool pantaloons and shirt. The weather was too rough to light the cabin stove, but the change of clothes revived his spirits somewhat. It was, after all, a privilege to be dry.

Luce settled into the upholstered chair behind the oak desk in his cabin. He smoothed his thick brown hair back and listlessly watched the dim light of the lantern suspended from the beam above him swing wildly as the ship pitched and yawed. He listened to the explosive reports when the bow slammed into a wave larger than most others. The creak and groan of wood mingled with the sounds of the storm outside. These long voyages for so many years had begun to wear him out. At the age of forty-three, with his birthday in April soon to make him yet another year older, the bashes across the Atlantic Ocean and back without time for much else had lost their luster.

During those hard days at sea he missed his second wife, Elizabeth, and his two sons, Robert, the elder, and Willie, a boy of just six. His first wife had died in labor back in 1836, after just three years of marriage, leaving him to raise Robert alone, until he met and married

Elizabeth Fearing two years later. Elizabeth was from Wareham, Massachusetts, the daughter of a wealthy landowner. She was well educated and kind. His love for her grew strong as the years passed, and their marriage of convenience became one of devotion. Six years earlier, Elizabeth gave birth to Willie.

Willie suffered from chronic pain due to an unknown ailment that left him crippled. He needed constant attention, and Luce had hired a manservant to tend to the boy's needs while he was gone, in addition to servants to help Elizabeth keep house. Willie made a brave effort to hide his discomfort, but the illness robbed him of even the simple pleasure of walking without assistance. He could not play with the other children he went to school with near their comfortable home out in the countryside of Yonkers, far from the bustle of Lower Manhattan. Luce missed his boy.

Luce had grown up in Rochester, Massachusetts. By the time he was nineteen, he had command of a small coastal trader, a young age for a master, even in those days. His quick wit and mild, social manner enabled him to climb the ranks without the usual brutality many of his colleagues employed. His crews respected his quiet reserve because they knew he would brook no laggards. In this, he was a different sort of captain, and he prided himself on it, though he knew some men along the waterfront considered him something of a dandy. While, according to newspapers of the time, he was a "thorough-going seaman," "well respected" and "held in the highest confidence" by his employers, he was far from the typical Yankee captain whom Lindsay described in his *History of Merchant Shipping:*

> As New England was the great storehouse of American seamen, there the best specimens of their seafaring population were to be found. We have seen, even in our time, the puritanical, weatherbeaten, Boston skipper—once so famous—sharp as a north-easter, dressed in knee-breeches and buckles, with a three-cornered cocked-hat, not forgetting the pigtail, the very

personification of our Commodore Trunnion and Piper of a century ago. But, though they may have degenerated since then, the seamen engaged in [the Atlantic trade] are still a remarkably hardy, robust race, and, hence, have succeeded in that branch of maritime enterprise far more than our own adventurers of late years.

Luce's decidedly civilized way of handling his packet crews may have worked well for him in the early days of his career. As Lindsay indicated, the vast majority of sailors hailed from New England and were quasi-literate and modestly upstanding. However, the rapid growth of the U.S. merchant marine in the late 1840s had led to a shortage of good men to serve before the mast. An increasing number of them were ruffians. The toughest of them all went into the transatlantic packet service and, in the 1850s, the clipper trade to California. Reports of discipline problems surfaced with alarming frequency during this period. The acts of brutality on the part of the captains and mates rose as well in a vicious circle that sometimes spun out of control.

One case in 1847, involving the packet *Columbia*, of the Black Ball Line, illustrates the trouble that sometimes arose when a hardened crew found themselves free of the influence of an officer's iron hand, a belaying pin, or a pistol clasped tight and ready. At the height of a winter gale in midocean, a rogue wave hurled the captain, the first and second officers, and several crewmen overboard. The third mate found himself pinned under the ship's wheel, helpless and in need of assistance. At this point, when they were needed most, a number of the men before the mast chose to mutiny. They terrorized the passengers and robbed the cabins, including the belongings of the captain, before distress signals brought the aid of another packet, whose master sent aboard a mate intimidating enough to restore order and bring the ship safely into port.

One packet captain, Samuel Samuels, quoted in Robert Albion's *Square-Riggers on Schedule*, wrote about his strong belief that civility had no place aboard a sailing vessel, especially one engaged in the New York–to–Liverpool trade:

> The Liverpool packet sailors were not easily demoralized. They were the toughest class of men in all respects. They could stand the worst weather, food, and usage, and put up with less sleep, more rum, and harder knocks than any other sailors. They would not sail in any other trade. They had not the slightest idea of morality or honesty, and gratitude was not in them. The dread of the belaying pin or heaver kept them in subjection. I tried to humanize these brutal natures as much as possible, but the better they were treated the more trouble my officers had with them.

Not all captains believed such tactics were needed, and Luce sided with them. A movement was on to bring law and order and moral decency to the merchant marine in the late 1840s and early 1850s. A chief lobbyist in this respect was the author Richard Henry Dana, Jr. The courts were more prone to listen to the grievances of sailors than ever before. Laws were passed to ensure crews had ample rations. Flogging was outlawed in the U.S. Navy in 1850, and it was illegal aboard merchant ships as well, though some captains did it anyway. The modern age awakening in America brought with it the belief that the base side of humanity should be expunged, that the moral fiber of the nation demanded a better way to behave toward its citizens. Luce was firmly rooted in this modern perception, but he was still in the minority among his colleagues.

As he reclined at his desk, lost in thoughts of the past and of home, he could not know that it was precisely his unique style of command, a combination of intelligence and gentlemanly demeanor, that would win him a chance to leap to the very fore of the U.S. merchant marine in a position coveted by the more than one hundred well-qualified skippers of the packets plying between New York and Great Britain and along the coast from Maine to the Gulf of Mexico. Of all these men, four would soon be given the opportunity to take command of a new breed of steamship, stamped with American ingenuity and backed with the might of the U.S. Treasury. These ships were already under construction in New York shipyards on the East River, and their sole purpose, in the words of the popular press, was to "cast this man Cunard from the sea."

CHAPTER TWO

SYMMETRY OF FORM

Dawn on January 28, 1850, slowly colored the sky over the warehouses and docks along the East River's Brooklyn shore and illuminated the thin clouds high above Long Island in brightening mauve turning to scarlet. Across the river in Manhattan, the city remained cloaked in shadows. The dull yellow glow of lamps in the windows of the three-story brick buildings on the waterfront revealed the presence of shopkeepers and clerks preparing for the day's business. The clop and clatter of horse-drawn drays and omnibuses crammed with workers echoed off the cobblestones as New York stirred awake. Ferries churned back and forth across the river, delivering additional cargoes of humanity.

Beyond the piers where packets, clippers, and coastal traders lay snugly to their berths, the footsteps and muffled whispers of laborers filled the air in the shipyards and ironworks in the northern outskirts of the city. The men rubbed sleep from their eyes, flexed their arms to drive away cramps made worse from winter's cold, and prepared to earn their daily wages. At the foot of Twelfth Street, at the shipyard of William H. Brown, the entire roster of employees arrived earlier than usual.

This day marked an important occasion for Brown's company. No fewer than three steamships perched on the ways ready for launch starting at nine-thirty sharp. Brown, a canny businessman, wanted to put on a show for New Yorkers. All of the best men and women from the wealthiest neighborhoods were expected to attend the launching of his latest masterpieces, *New World, Boston,* and most impressive of all, *Arctic,* a massive steamship built for the Collins Line. To add to the spectacle, Brown intended to send *New World* sliding down the ways with a full head of steam up, enabling her to engage her paddle wheels when the ship's hull hit the water and proceed immediately on a shakedown cruise around the upper bay. No builder had ever done that before, mostly because it was considered dangerous. But Brown's reputation depended on keeping his name in the newspapers and cultivating the attention of the wealthiest merchants and shipowners in New York, and he knew how to please crowds.

The spectators began arriving in Brown's yard as early as eight o'clock as the yard's workers greased the ways with tallow to provide a slick surface for the ships to slide down into the East River. The men set about preparing to knock the stout wooden wedges out from beneath the hulls to start the steamers on their quick journeys to the river. As each wedge was removed, the weight of the ship bore down on the supporting structure set at an angle facing the water's edge. Other laborers readied the yard for the crowd. They cleared away the scatter of timber and tools so people could gather with the least number of obstructions to clutter the view.

Adjacent to Brown's yard was the busy Stillman, Allen and Company, commonly referred to as the Novelty Iron Works. There the mammoth, nearly two-story-high side-lever marine engines of *Arctic* were already under construction at the tremendous expense of $250,000, amounting to more than one-third of the ship's total $700,000 cost. The steamship *Atlantic,* the first of the four ships of the Collins Line, lay to her moorings at Novelty's quays as the installation of her steam engines continued. The manager of the Collins Line, officially the United States Mail Steamship Company, was Edward Knight Collins. Every bit as much a showman as Brown, Collins knew how to grab a crowd better than almost any other man in New York City. He arranged to use *Atlantic* as a grandstand for the day's events and issued tickets to a select group of well-heeled New Yorkers.

In addition to members of high society, Collins asked the elite packet captains to attend. As yet, no masters had been named for the prized commands of the four liners. Most, if not all, of the captains wanted to seize the promising opportunity for themselves. Well known to Collins and a friend of the banking family who put up a substantial sum of the initial capital for the venture, Captain Luce knew he was a strong contender.

Collins sent invitations to the press as well, including the shipping reporter for the *New York Herald.* James Gordon Bennett, publisher of the newspaper, took a special interest in maritime matters. The fortunes of the metropolis were closely linked to the sea and the ability of the U.S. merchant marine to outperform its British competitors. Not all publishers in Manhattan supported the Collins Line, however. Reporters from the *New York Evening Post* were not invited to view the launchings from *Atlantic* because of its frequent editorials questioning whether the U.S. government should spend public money to subsidize a private enterprise. The *Post* sided with the owners of the sailing packets who objected to the subsidies Collins had secured from Congress. Lindsay described the consternation of the opposing parties in his 1870s history of the merchant marine:

> Moreover, it was urged, in favour of the principle of subsidies, that the American sailing packets, though undoubtedly vessels of unrivalled beauty and swiftness, were fast losing the most valuable portion of their trade through the competition of steamers under a foreign flag; but, so far from this being an argument in favour of establishing vessels of their own of a similar description, the shipowners of New York and Boston and in all the leading American ports, who held the sailing-ships as a property, naturally complained that the United States' Government should improperly interfere by a protective system, which would inflict a double injury upon them, and insisted that such matters should be left entirely to individual enterprise, which, in their opinion, becomes paralyzed under the ef-

fects of Government patronage bestowed upon some to the exclusion of others.

Despite protests in the press from certain publishers and objections from special interest groups, Congress chose to fight Cunard and his British backers with a New York–to–Liverpool line funded in part with public money. It was thought that the building of the four steamships for the Collins Line—*Atlantic, Pacific, Arctic,* and *Baltic*—represented America's best hope to reassert supremacy in maritime commerce and break Cunard's monopoly on carrying the mail between England and the United States. A fifth ship was part of the original proposal for the line, but due to cost overruns construction was put off for the future.

The contract was awarded to Edward Knight Collins, and his two main backers, James and Stewart Brown, of a prominent banking family who owned Brown Brothers and Company on Wall Street. Together with some smaller stockholders, Collins and the Browns raised an initial $1.2 million to capitalize the venture and began work to execute their contract with the United States, which was signed on November 1, 1847. The subsidy of $385,000 per year stipulated that Collins's steamers would carry mail on twenty round-trip crossings per year—twice each month in spring, summer, and fall and once a month in winter.

At an average of 280 feet in length, 2,800 tons by custom house measurement, and powered with engines of 1,000 horsepower each, Collins's ships were designed to outclass Cunard's in every way. They were bigger, faster, and far more luxurious, or at least that was what the politicians and the general public expected. Whether Collins might succeed in delivering on his promises remained subject to actual performance, but hopes ran high in most quarters that this line of steamships would at last restore national pride in the U.S. merchant marine. *Atlantic* and *Pacific* were nearly ready for sea. *Arctic* was expected to sail in the autumn of 1850, as was *Baltic*.

The Collins steamships represented the first real steps forward in efforts of the United States to assert itself as a naval power in the dawn of the modern age that steam had already brought about in Europe. These ships were built not only for commerce but for quick and easy conversion to warships. Framed in oak and planked with pine, iron reinforced the structural integrity of each vessel. Cunard's steamers were also built for use in time of war, and in a very real sense the Collins and other lines of steamships granted subsidies from the U.S. Treasury amounted to an arms race, a push to stay on an equal footing with Great Britain from a tactical and strategic perspective.

James Alexander Hamilton, son of Alexander Hamilton, first secretary of the treasury of the United States, was one of the more outspoken public figures who viewed the British advances in steamship development with deep mistrust and burgeoning anxiety. On February 22, 1841, in the last days of the Van Buren administration, he wrote the following letter from New York to Senator Daniel Webster, soon to be secretary of state, who shared his nationalistic point of view.

Dear Sir:—I have the honor to inclose a letter containing information which seems to me clearly to indicate that Great Britain is preparing to increase her lake armaments. . . . Two or three years ago I sent Mr. Van Buren a statement of the actual condition of the Steam Marine of Great Britain, and intimated to him as worthy of consideration that the employment of this new agent in this manner and to the extent of navigating the ocean had perhaps rendered it necessary to revise our system of coast defences, the position of forts, and to defend our harbors which are to be attacked. Sail ships might be wholly useless where steam vessels are employed, from considerations that will be so obvious to you as to forbid their repetition. . . .

Cunard's steamers, drawing twelve feet water, could be made to carry two large guns to 10-inch balls of 90 lbs. each, and four or six smaller ones. Take the case of Newport harbor. The entrance upon which our fort is to bear is wide, deep, open, and accessible to vessels of all sizes, but there is another entrance around the island which carries throughout twelve feet water, although very narrow. Such vessels as Cunard's steamers can navigate it; and thus command the towns of Newport and Providence with the adjoining country, regardless of our present fortresses.

So it was against this perceived double threat from Great Britain, economic and military, that the more than 30,000 spectators gathered in and around William H. Brown's yard on that cold January morning. They were there to express their patriotism as much as they were to witness the launch of Collins's third example of hoped-for American superiority over the British. *Arctic*'s sheer size and "symmetry of form" inspired admiration among the onlookers.

Like her sisters, *Arctic* was the creation of one of New York's most innovative naval architects, a young man of only twenty-nine by the name of George Steers. Steers, a tall, quiet fellow, was well known for his work designing the fastest of the swift pilot boats that made New York famous on both sides of the Atlantic Ocean, as well as the racing yachts for the wealthy members of the New York Yacht Club. He was a close friend of Collins, who admired his unique approach to naval architecture.

In his work on the Collins ships, Steers eliminated the sweep of the clipper bow, with its long bowsprit and jibboom so common on most other steamships of the day. The bows of the Collins ships were nearly plumb, or a straight vertical line from the forecastle deck to the cutwater, where the ship sliced through the waves. As with his future work on yacht *America* in the fall of 1850, his innovations were much ahead of his time. He did not do away with sails completely. The Collins ships were bark-rigged with three masts. The fore and main masts carried traditional square sails, and the mizzenmast carried a large fore-and-aft sail known as a spanker. (The mizzenmasts were removed in 1853 to improve steering performance.) But Steers did reduce the sail area to make the canvas more an auxiliary mode of propulsion, another major departure from traditional steamship designs. The sterns he rounded at the transom, giving the liners a graceful appearance from that quarter. Like the sailing vessels he designed, Steers created a model for the Collins ships with speed at the forefront of his consider-ations.

At 2,856 tons by American custom house measurement and 284 feet in length, *Arctic* stood on the ways as high as a three-story build-ing, her sleek, black hull smooth and shiny enough to reflect light. From the ground, viewers could make out the tops of the white deck-houses, which would contain the dining, main, and ladies' saloons and the men's smoking room, all areas of princely luxury spacious enough to accommodate more than two hundred passengers. Below these upper structures were four decks for the first- and second-class state-rooms, quarters for the crew, the hold, and the engine machinery mounted on a massive iron bed affixed to the bottom of the hull. More easily discerned from a distance was the tall black protrusion of her smokestack, its red top marking her as a Collins ship.

Amidships on each side of the hull, a giant wrought iron wheel just over thirty-five feet wide lay half-hidden behind a half-moon-shaped paddle-wheel box painted black and adorned with carved golden shields of the United States. Attached to the wheel were a series of wooden floats, bucket-like fittings made to catch water similar to any found on the wheel of a grist mill. The lower edge of the wheel ex-tended seven feet below the waterline against the bright copper sheathing that protected the wood from marine borers and retarded the growth of barnacles and slime.

At precisely nine-thirty, the first of the launchings commenced as *New World* and then *Boston* splashed into the East River to the "loud cheering and huzzahs of the assembled multitude," the reporter from the *New York Herald* wrote the next day, January 29. The attention of the crowd, which numbered approximately 6 percent of the entire population of New York City, turned to *Arctic*. Thanks to Edward Knight Collins, the reporter from the *Herald* occupied a perfect vantage point from which to witness the launch of *Arctic*. He described what happened next:

> Those two launches being over, it was evident that the third and greatest one of all, that of the steamship Arctic, might be expected to take place every moment. There she lay . . . poised, as it were, in the air, the centre of attention and the object of a laudable pride to every one present who took an interest in American progress and desired to see the United States stand at the head of the nations in everything that tends to promote civilization. . . .
>
> Anon, the wedges which held her were one by one removed—she moved slightly, as if awaking from a long repose—and then she bowed and slipped into her native element . . . men waved their hats, the ladies their handkerchiefs, in admiration of the glad event. Away she shot across the river, fully two-thirds of the distance to the opposite shore and the two little steamers that were in readiness to take her in tow, proceeded after her to bring her to dock. She presented a magnificent appearance in the water. Then it was that her immense size, and the beauty and symmetry of her model, were displayed to advantage.
>
> Instead of the thousands who witnessed her launch turning their backs and proceeding to their homes as soon as she dipped into the water, as is generally the case, hardly one moved, all kept the positions which they had previously occupied, and for nearly half an hour stood contemplating the splendid vessel. At the end of that time, the vast multitude dispersed, each taking another look at the noble ship before leaving.

Much work remained to be done before *Arctic* lifted her bow to the ocean swells for the first time. For months, the engineers at the Novelty Iron Works fitted the ship out with the great machines that promised the speedy passages to come, and carpenters, painters, and riggers completed the tasks associated with their trades to make her ready for sea. As she neared completion, she seemed to take on a spirit of her own.

Among her admirers was Captain Luce, whom Edward Knight Collins had named as the ship's master after her launch in January. Luce followed the last phases of her construction with a focus typical of his character. He appreciated his duty. But more than that, *Arctic* represented the culmination of all he had struggled to achieve since his boyhood. The spring and summer of 1850 passed, and Luce was drawn from one world to another, from sail to steam, from a precarious future to one that looked brighter than ever before.

In just four years, he would become, in the words of the *New York Herald,* the "most famous and most miserable man in America."

CHAPTER THREE

SEA TRIAL

A BRISK NORTHERLY BREEZE kicked up a slight chop on the North River, as the Hudson River was called in previous centuries, and carried out over the wide expanse of the upper bay the odor of fish, horse manure, and the ever-present hints of coal and wood smoke from the thousands of stoves needed to heat the buildings of the city. All manner of small craft darted about the sailing ships at anchor off Governors Island. Steam ferries thrashed across the river back and forth to Hoboken, while others bound for Long Island Sound made their way up the East River as the last of the flood tide swept inland from the sea.

Directly across from the southern tip of Manhattan Island in Jersey City, the brand-new piers of the Cunard Company presented a scene of busy activity, as they had since 1848. Stevedores and longshoremen loaded freight into the holds of the steamships. Passengers gathered with their luggage, ready to check it with the cabin attendants before boarding. U.S. Post Office employees trundled bags of mail down to the docks just prior to sailing. Although *Atlantic* and *Pacific* of the Collins Line had been in service since the spring and carried their share of the mail, the Cunarders still were entitled to transport it, and they continued to do so with their usual regularity. However, the days of Cunard's unchallenged monopoly had officially ended on April 27, 1850, when *Atlantic* set sail on her maiden voyage from New York under the command of James West.

On the Manhattan side of the North River, the American mail ships of Edward Knight Collins dwarfed those of Cunard. Lying bow to in her berth, the forecastle deck of *Arctic* pointed directly at the waterfront along Canal Street, her stern to the British rivals across the river. Perhaps it was due to space and convenience that Collins established his dockage for the line in plain sight of Cunard's vast facilities in New Jersey, and no doubt the less fierce tidal currents of the North River, compared to those of the notorious East River, factored into the decision. But regardless of the reasons for its placement, the Collins depot seemed to stand in pugnacious defiance of Cunard, a symbol of American will to win back the position of prominence on the high seas. Just as the United States and Great Britain peered across the broad Atlantic at each other with less than friendly sentiments, so too did the agents of Edward Knight Collins and Samuel Cunard from their respective territories on the banks of the North River.

Steamship *Arctic* made an imposing sight. She caught the eye of the river boatmen and the skippers of the slow, lumbering sloops that plied the waters of the North River between Albany and Manhattan. Of all the Collins liners, she was the largest and most luxurious, and by all accounts on both sides of the Atlantic, she was considered the queen of the world's top class of oceangoing steam vessels. British merchant W. S. Lindsay noted, "The Arctic was considered the finest of the fleet, familiarly known as the 'clipper of the seas.' . . . Her equipment was complete and of the highest order, as I can testify from inspection, while her cabin accommodation in comfort and elegance surpassed that of any merchant vessel Great Britain then possessed."

Dense black smoke poured from *Arctic*'s funnel and whipped away in the breeze. Down below, a full complement of ten engineers, their assistants, twenty-four coal heavers, and twenty-four firemen were on hand to fire the boilers and tend the engines. Members of the Novelty Iron Works team of mechanics and advisers assisted them, showing them the workings and maintenance of *Arctic*'s power plants as they prepared to take her out on her first trial of speed, an overnight cruise to nowhere on October 18 and 19. Above deck, thirty-eight sailors under the command of the first officer climbed the rigging out onto the yards to let go the gaskets and unfurl the square sails. The ship bustled with men and rang with the shouts of orders from the officers.

Standing apart, but in command of the commotion through his officers, Captain Luce leaned against the brass life rail mounted at the uppermost curve of *Arctic*'s portside paddle-wheel box. As the highest and least obstructed locations aboard the steamship aside from the smokestack and the masts, the paddle-wheel boxes represented the equivalent of a modern ship's bridge. They were the province of the officers, places as revered as the poop deck of his last command, *Constellation,* which he had given up when Collins tapped him as one of the four luckiest captains in the U.S. merchant marine. Luce surveyed the river traffic. With the knowledge that he was about to execute the complicated maneuver of conning a big ship from the safety of her berth, he judged the state of the slackening tide and the strength of the sustained wind and the gusts, and thought carefully about his next move.

He was an experienced captain and had taken ships from their berths hundreds of times. Yet he was wise enough to know that the sea remained unpredictable, and with an untried ship, the odds for trouble increased dramatically. Two steam tenders held station a short distance away in case the engines suddenly failed, but like any other captain, Luce no doubt hoped no emergencies would make assistance necessary. He was still becoming accustomed to commanding a steamship.

Facing the bow, Luce would have noted that the wind pushed *Arctic* away from the pier on the left side of the ship, putting a strain on the cables on that side. Although he could not see the ones to starboard because the deckhouses obstructed his view, he knew they hung slack. These he would let go first. Luce called down to the mate on deck below, First Officer Robert Gourlay. He stood abaft the paddle-wheel box ready to activate the bell signals that communicated the captain's orders to the engine room and the helmsman in the wheelhouse, who could see nothing forward. The ship's deckhouses blocked his field of vision. He steered a blind course, following only the compass situated in front of him and relying on the officer atop the paddle-wheel box to guide him.

"Cast off starboard cables, Mister Gourlay!" he called down to the mate, a burly mariner intelligent in the ways of handling sailors.

"Cast off starboard, aye!" Gourlay replied. He passed the orders to the crewmen. Dockhands on the pier threw the lines into the river, a succession of splashes marking their progress. Teams of *Arctic*'s crew hauled the lines aboard and coiled them neatly on deck one by one.

"Slack off port cables!" Luce shouted. Gourlay repeated the order to indicate to Luce he had heard him correctly and directed the deckhands to ease off the lines that were taut from the weight of the ship as the wind came in full on the port beam. Immediately, *Arctic* stirred in her berth and moved sideways to clearer water away from the quays on either side. "We'll keep tension on the forward bow line, Mister Gourlay. Let it go when I say," Luce said.

Luce ordered the engines slow astern. Below in the engine room, the signal bell to reverse clanged near the control platform, upon which stood the chief engineer orchestrating the actions of every man under his command. Although the engines of the steamship were huge, weighing 750 tons, and were fired with a double row of furnaces and four boilers capable of holding 150 tons of water drawn directly from the sea for conversion into steam, the complex network of interconnected machinery worked quietly enough to communicate without shouting. The engineer ordered his assistants to put the engines into reverse and give them power. The levers, rods, valves, and pistons began to move, and the heavy crankshafts of the wheels spun slowly. The side-wheels came to life and washed the water against the hull into a welter of hissing white foam.

Luce gripped the life rail lightly as he moved fore and aft on the paddle-wheel box, his eyes seeming to be everywhere at once. *Arctic* backed out of her berth. He shouted to cast off stern lines and fore and aft spring lines, and to hold steady on the forward bow line to keep the ship's bow from paying off too rapidly in the wind. A gust hit the steamer. The sailors at the bitts put their weight into holding the bow line taut, until the vessel had way on and it was safe to cast off. In the space of a few minutes, *Arctic* was free of her tethers to the land and headed southward down the bay toward the Verrazano Narrows and the open ocean beyond Sandy Hook. Once away from the dock, one of the best men from the Sandy Hook Pilots, an association of mariners who by law were to be present to guide ships in and out of port, ascended the stairs leading up to the paddle-wheel box and stood beside Captain Luce.

"She swims well, Captain," the pilot said.

The tension ebbed. "Aye, she does indeed," Luce replied, the crow's-feet at the corners of his eyes pinching tight, the creases of his tanned face deepening.

Luce leaned over the rail and observed Gourlay, and noted a large grin on the mate's face. The first time a ship got under way marked the real start of her life, and everyone aboard knew it. "We'll make sail now, Mister Gourlay!"

As the sails, already in their gear, were pulled down from the yards like curtains and the topsail and royal yards were raised, the canvas boomed and suddenly went tight with a belly under the press of the breeze. Almost simultaneously, the crew at the foremast raised the headsails while their counterparts at the mizzenmast unbrailed the spanker and eased the sheet to let the sail out for maximum exposure to the wind.

Arctic picked up speed, though her engines turned out just enough power to revolve the side-wheels at half the revolutions needed for full ahead. The eddies and whirls of her wake cut a slick in the chop of the river. Hearing the rhythmic slap of the paddle wheels and feeling the subtle vibration of the engines far below his feet struck Luce as a bit odd. The ship exuded a power altogether different from that of a sailing packet, which moved through the seas with only the murmur of the bow wave, the hum of the taut rigging, and the creak and groan of wood as the vessel flexed with the ocean. The steamship achieved her own harmony, though it was not as pleasing to a sailor like Luce as the grace of a full-rigged packet making her way out of the harbor at the heels of a fair northerly wind. Soon enough the motion of the steamship, her own set of sounds and smells, would become as ordinary to him as what he was used to aboard the sailing ships he had commanded for twenty-six years. But the modern age, despite its financial rewards, would take some adjusting to.

The ship safely under way, Luce let the pilot take over the command until they were beyond the shoals of Sandy Hook bar at the seaward approaches to Gedney Channel. Gazing out at the harbor from his vantage point high above the dark water swirling past under the paddle wheels, he might have reflected that in all his years at sea, 1850 remained a high point, one that had swiftly changed his prospects for the future to a distinctly brighter hue with his enormous salary of $6,000 per year, the equivalent of $108,000 today. The captains of the Collins Line were among the highest-paid mariners of the 1850s, a matter of pride for the company's manager, Edward Knight Collins.

Collins was just three years older than Luce, and but for the fortunes of fate, both men might have shared a common career path. Both hailed from Massachusetts and from an early age had found the sea a compelling influence that drew them to it with an inexorable power. But where Luce chose command, Collins chose the counting-house. After a brief stint at sea himself to become acquainted with the men and ships he later commissioned, he ran his mercantile business with his father, Israel Gross Collins, before branching off on his own after his father's death in 1831.

In 1827, when the packets were on the rise, Collins and his father began to operate a small line of ships to Vera Cruz on the Gulf of Mexico. The firm remained diminutive in comparison to the Black Ball, Red Star, and Swallowtail lines serving the transatlantic trade, but it prospered well enough under Collins's management to attract the attention of the main backers of a New York company regularly dispatching vessels to New Orleans. It was in the coastal trade that Collins learned the business of administering a packet line, and he soon adopted the strategy of defeating competitors with bigger, faster, and more luxurious ships.

In 1835, Collins turned his attention to the more lucrative transatlantic trade. His Dramatic Line, a fleet of large packets named after theatrical figures and personalities, included *Shakespeare, Garrick, Sheridan, Siddons,* and *Roscius,* the last being the first packet to exceed 1,000 tons. *Roscius* cost Collins a fortune to build, and his competitors scoffed, dubbing the ship "Collins's Folly." But his belief that the traveling public would favor large, luxurious ships proved correct. *Roscius* became one of the fastest of the New York packets and earned back her construction costs many times over.

Collins's choice of Luce to command *Arctic* was well informed and reasonable. Luce's record in the merchant marine spoke for itself, but that did not account entirely for his choice; there were many other captains with similarly lustrous qualifications. Luce was a well-known figure among the merchants of New York for his affable manner, intelligence, and social skills. He could talk with the wealthiest of men and women and yet command the respect of sailors before the mast. Not every packet captain possessed these benefits of civilization. Many, in fact, were hardly more civilized than the lowliest of their crew. They simply had power, the knowledge of navigation, and a knack for mathematics their subordinates lacked. Such men would not suit Collins. He needed captains who would follow his orders to steam full ahead regardless of adversities of weather, be they fog or storm, while at the same time playing host to the first-class passengers as a representative of not only the company but of the United States as well—a kind of maritime ambassador.

As the hills of Staten Island passed to starboard while the pilot guided *Arctic* down the Main Ship Channel toward Sandy Hook, Luce might have felt the strain of being suddenly elevated to such a prestigious command. He found himself caught up in what the newspapers of the city dubbed the Great Atlantic Race, a push for speed at all costs to outshine the vessels of Samuel Cunard. *Atlantic* and *Pacific* had made eight voyages since the line went into service in April 1850, and five of the eastbound crossings had been done in just over ten days, a feat remarked on in the press with admiration and a crowing declaration of national pride. Much was expected of Luce. In just eight days, *Arctic* was scheduled to sail on her maiden transatlantic voyage.

On the day of departure, October 26, 1850, as Luce supervised the final loading of *Arctic*'s cargo and the embarkation of the passengers, readers of the *New York Herald* opened the pages of the newspaper to the following announcement:

> The magnificent steamship Arctic, the third of the Collins' splendid line, will leave here today, at noon, for Liverpool. We gave an account a few days since of her trial trip, and then expressed an opinion, that if she did not at least equal the Atlantic and Pacific, the pioneers of this line, we would be very much astonished. . . . If we are not very much mistaken, the day will soon come when it will be considered a long trip if these vessels do not make the passage, as a general thing, in less than ten days. E. K. Collins is a man whose energy is unbounded, whose skills unquestioned, and whose ambition keeps pace with his energy. At one bound he jumped into successful rivalry with the Old World in the matter of steam navigation—in another he will leave all competitors far behind. He thinks, like all other good Americans, that the United States should be without a rival in everything.

Crowds gathered on the docks at Canal Street to see *Arctic* off. Relatives of the passengers embraced and some of them wept, wishing their loved ones Godspeed and a safe passage, as the hour of noon drew near and the crew prepared to cast off *Arctic*'s warps and proceed to sea. Luce stood on the paddle-wheel box, his mind focused on the business of working the vessel. She backed from her berth out into the harbor, and sailors at the bow fired the customary two-gun salute from her signal cannon. Gray smoke carried away in the wind. The reports echoed off the buildings on the waterfront to the cheers of spectators. He had a good crew, a stout ship, and an ocean to cross. Just how fast he might manage to do it remained an open question, given the capricious nature of the Atlantic and all it could muster to defy human ingenuity. The sea was an unforgiving body of water capable of inflicting great harm on those who ventured across it. Luce, who had never lost a ship in all his days of command, would find out soon enough how deadly it could be.

CHAPTER FOUR

SPEED AT
ALL COSTS

O N HER FIRST VOYAGE in October 1850, *Arctic* performed well and without incident, a welcome outcome even if she did not break any records. Her sister ship *Atlantic* was not so lucky on her maiden transatlantic journey. Steaming out of New York Harbor on April 27, 1850, she hit ice and damaged one of her paddle wheels. She made it to Liverpool in thirteen days, a slow passage. But the ships of the Collins Line soon proved that a ten-day crossing was routine, and *Arctic* met and exceeded these expectations with numerous transits of the Atlantic Ocean in nine days. By the early spring of 1852, *Arctic* had proven herself as one of the fastest ocean liners in the world.

As she set out on her ninth passage on March 20, 1852, a fair wind from the north enabled the steamer to carry full sail out past Nantucket Shoals. She headed eastward at top speed toward Nova Scotia on the great circle route that would take her on the most direct path to Liverpool. That path was not a straight line from Sandy Hook to Cape Clear, off the south coast of Ireland, where she would turn northward into the Irish Sea to reach Liverpool, but more a long bend that was actually shorter because it followed the curvature of the earth.

Unlike the sailing packets Luce had commanded, which required him to set a course more with the winds and current of the Gulf Stream in mind, he was free aboard *Arctic* to set a precision heading, a true conformance to the great circle route that cut the voyages from a typical 3,137 nautical miles for a ship under sail to just 3,055 for a steamship, thus reaping the rewards of powerful engines and a shorter overall distance to make good between ports. A clear blue sky reflected off the waves, coloring them a deep aquamarine dappled with the sparkle of sunlight unobscured with the shadows of passing clouds. He enjoyed the bracing cold weather and counted himself blessed with the ease with which he could obtain his celestial observations with the sextant. He and First Officer Gourlay took the sights together in the morning, at noon (when they determined their latitude), and in the afternoon to keep a running fix to use in deducing the ship's position as she moved swiftly through the seas.

On these chilly early spring voyages, the ship sailed with few customers paying the one-way first-class fare of $130, the equivalent of $2,340 today. That $130 amounted roughly to a year's pay for sailors serving before the mast on average merchant vessels of the day, and a round-trip ticket equaled the annual wages of schoolteachers, clerks, and laborers. However, aboard the Collins ships, the entire crew was paid well above fair market prices for their services. Luce and his fellow commanders hand-picked their crews and chose only the very best men for the job. The average payroll per month for each of the four liners ran in excess of $4,500, excluding the princely sums paid to the masters: James C. Luce of *Arctic,* James West of *Atlantic,* Joseph Comstock of *Baltic,* and Ezra Nye of *Pacific.*

The height of the transatlantic passenger season did not begin until May, when the waters of the North Atlantic calmed down and the wealthy residents of New York and denizens of high society from other cities jaunted off to Europe. During the summer months through September, steamships brought thousands of people back and forth across the ocean. After that, the gales of winter roared in and discouraged all but the hardiest of travelers. These off-season voyagers were usually those required to make the journey for business reasons. Of the 180 souls aboard *Arctic* on that March passage of 1852, only 51 were passengers.

The passengers soon found their sea legs, or at least they attempted to do so. They ate four-course dinners in the palatial dining saloon without the usual din when it was packed with more than two hundred diners. The numerous empty tables along the sixty-two-foot length of the room presented an odd, almost deserted ambiance. Luce welcomed these occasions. Although he found the socializing that was part of his job agreeable, the break from the usual constant banter proved relaxing.

The main saloon was relatively sparse in population, its 100-foot length seemingly larger with the paucity of occupants. Luce visited with the small groups of men and women lounging on the sofas and in armchairs, talking quietly, playing cards, or reading. Windows overlooking the sea two stories below afforded an abundance of natural light that bathed the polished satinwood and rosewood walls, and the paintings featuring the coats of arms of various states of the Union, the lush, thick carpets on the hardwood floors, the cool white surface of the marble tabletops, the mirrors and stained glass, and gilt work throughout. Steam radiators heated all the spaces aboard, and many of the passengers commented that these were most-appreciated fixtures.

The foul east wind came in on the night of March 21, just thirty hours into the voyage. The sky filled with dark, low clouds. Waves built, and *Arctic* began to pitch as she steamed straight into them, sending sheets of spray flying over the forecastle deck aft along the promenade deck adjacent to the dining, main, and ladies' saloons, as well as the men's smoking room at the stern. The wind and seas built steadily and showed no signs of diminishing. As the captain, Luce was not required to stand watch on the exposed catwalks on top of the paddle-wheel boxes, but his officers did have to, and it was tough duty in bad weather.

In the words of Richard Henry Dana, Jr., in his book *The Seaman's Friend*, published in 1851, "Where there are passengers, as in a regular line of packet ships (or, as they are familiarly called, *liners*,) between New York and Liverpool or Havre, for instance, the master has even less to do with the day's work; since the navigation and working of the ship, with proper attention to his passengers, is as much as can reasonably be required of him. . . . As the master stands no watch, he comes and goes as he pleases, and takes his own hours for rest."

A great deal was left up to the discretion of the captain when it came to working the ship. Some chose to remain aloof and apart, others acted as tyrants, and a lesser number maintained discipline by more civil means of working hard to build a team of loyal officers and crew through setting a personal example of character and an industrious nature. Luce, being of the last sort, saw no reason that he should not share in the unpleasantness of duty on the paddle-wheel box to spell his officers on occasion to let them drink a cup of hot coffee in the chart house or enjoy a smoke in the men's smoking room.

Bucking the storm reduced *Arctic*'s usual speed of thirteen knots to just nine or ten, about the average cruising speed of the majority of Cunard's steamers. Luce kept the engines at full power in his battle for fast passages regardless of the weather. However, in this unusual easterly wind, the high speed caused the ship to pound. She lifted her bow to the waves, soared skyward, and crashed down on top of the next crest with stupendous force. The men below in the engine room and those passing coal from the bunkers to the firemen at the furnaces struggled to keep their footing and avoid breaking bones or suffering severe burns. *Arctic* consumed approximately eighty-five tons of coal every day, and her four boilers needed 8,000 gallons of seawater per hour to evaporate into steam. The forty-eight coal heavers and firemen, in addition to the engineering staff, worked shifts of eight hours each. It was hot and dirty work. These men were known as the black gang—oil and grease smeared their faces, hands, and coveralls—and they were among the toughest members of the merchant marine.

The rough weather presented a challenge to the thirty-eight cooks, stewards, waiters, and other housekeeping staff. In the galley, pots and pans threatened to make their contents fly. The cast-iron stoves became dangerous to anyone standing near them. A violent lurch of the vessel meant almost certain injury. The waiters carrying platters loaded with food and drink assumed a ballet-like choreography as they served the diners their five meals per day: breakfast at eight, lunch at noon, dinner at half past three, tea at seven, and supper at ten. In between meals, the men, and some of the ladies, dulled their misery or boredom with fine wines, champagne, and hard liquor. The waiters never stopped working during their shifts. They scurried from the bar or galley (kitchen) with drinks and food, cleared away the glasses and dishes when the passengers left, and began the whole cycle again when others sat down at the tables.

Aboard *Arctic* was a reporter for *Harper's New Monthly Magazine*, a preacher named John S. C. Abbott. Luce tried to make him feel at home, though the writer expressed some concern and weariness about the protracted storm. Abbott recalled in his article a visit with Luce in the comfortable environs of the ladies' saloon:

> In the boudoir-like magnificence of the ladies' saloon, with our excellent captain, and a few intelligent and pleasant companions, gentlemen and ladies, we almost forgot, for an hour, the storm and the gloom without, and conversed with just as much joyousness as if we had been in the most luxurious parlor on land. These saloons, brilliantly lighted with carcel lamps, look far more gorgeous and imposing by night than by day. It is now eleven o'clock at night. Every other moment an enormous billow lifts us high into the air, and then we go down, down, down, exciting that peculiar sensation which I remember often to have had in my dreams when a child.

Abbott went on to say, "By [Captain Luce's] social qualities, and his untiring vigilance, he won the esteem of all in the ship. . . . I have only to add, that, if you ever wish to cross the Atlantic, you will find in the Arctic one of the noblest of ships, and in Captain Luce one of the best of commanders."

The storm began to weigh more heavily on Luce as it dragged on, slowing the ship even further and consuming large amounts of expensive coal. The gloom and fatigue mixed with his worry about the very existence of the Collins Line and, by extension, the position of his own personal fortunes. Willie's illness cost a lot of money in doctors' fees and wages for his manservant. The house in Yonkers required ample funds to maintain, and Robert was soon to be off to college, yet another financial responsibility. The Collins Line might fold if it was not able to turn a profit soon, and thus far it had not. What then? There was no future in any oceangoing vessel not powered by steam.

Although the line had succeeded in large part in its objective of besting the ships of Samuel Cunard, it had done so at a substantial financial cost. In spite of the fact that the Collins ships had reduced Cunard's share of market in fine freight and first-class passengers by more than 50 percent, each voyage the Collins liners made incurred a deficit of approximately $17,000, while Cunard's books remained consistently in the black. The high speeds required to outperform Cunard added huge expenses in the extra coal needed to achieve those fast passages. The bill for coal alone on each trip amounted to $10,000 or more. The sumptuous menus, part of the $130 fares, reduced profit potential. The wages for officers and crews soared above those Cunard was paying. A master of a Cunard steamship received an annual salary of only $2,500, compared to the $6,000 Luce and his colleagues were paid. The Great Atlantic Race came with a price tag in dollars and cents that struck many as wasteful, though they were still in the minority in 1852.

Among the more vocal detractors was the *New York Evening Post*, an old enemy of Collins. On February 22, 1852, James Gordon Bennett of the *Herald* blasted his peers at the *Post* with the following editorial:

> For some time past, the *Evening Post*, one of the most vindictive, unscrupulous, unprincipled organs of the old Van Buren abolition faction of New York, has been engaged in making attacks, assaults and misrepresentations upon the Collins line of

steamers, and, indeed, all other steam lines in which the government have a connection, either to California or to Europe. The arguments presented by this opposition are a mixture of arithmetic and malice—a slice of commercial figuring and political hostility, curiously interwoven with each other, as despair and revenge are mixed up with the character of Satan in the Bible and Paradise Lost.

The system on which the United States government have established many of the Post Office steam lines, does not acquire its necessity and utility from the advantages it confers on commerce or social intercourse alone. Our great mail steam system is the incipient step for the building and equipment of a great steam navy, always ready for action in any international emergency, without the necessity of expending millions of dormant capital in order to be so prepared. At any moment the mail steam navy of the United States can be converted into an efficient arm of the government.

The *Herald* and other pro-Collins newspapers in the United States continued to trumpet the fast passages of the Collins ships—how they had in fact "cast Cunard from the sea." There were indeed some glorious moments that even the opposition admitted did much to enhance national esteem and honor on the global stage. The previous August, *Baltic* had stunned the world when she made the run from Liverpool to New York in just nine days, thirteen hours, and fifty minutes. Up to August 1851, no liner had ever made a faster westbound passage. Newspapers all over the United States and Europe carried the story. Captain Luce had added to the celebrations on his previous passage in February 1852, making the eastbound run to Liverpool in just nine days, seventeen hours, and twelve minutes, a record that won him much praise and public adulation.

But while these exceptional passages captured the imaginations and fanned the national pride of Americans, Collins was savvy enough

Record-Setting Passage of Steamship *Arctic*, 1852

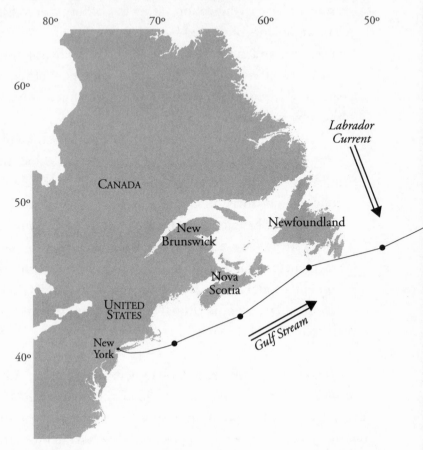

to scrutinize all the numbers and come up with a more realistic assessment. In a meeting with his captains, he went over the records for 1851. The Cunard steamships actually outdid those of the Collins Line on the eastbound run, arriving in Liverpool an average of one hour, forty-eight minutes ahead. No doubt part of the reason for this rested on the larger sail area of the Cunard liners, which took greater advantage of the prevailing westerly winds, and simple good luck with the weather. The Collins ships did better than Cunard's on the westbound run against the westerlies, arriving an average of nearly *sixteen hours* ahead. Both lines were racking up ten- and eleven-day runs as a

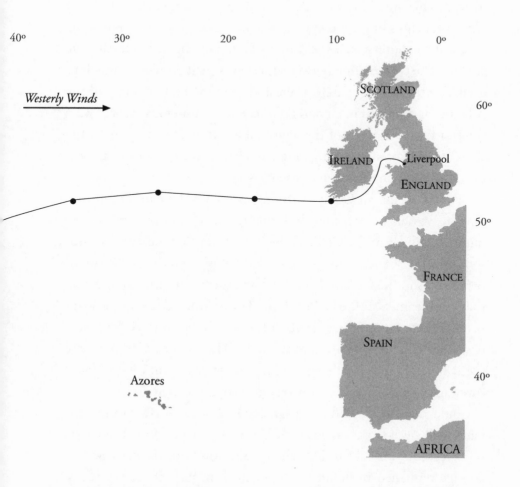

matter of routine. Collins fumed about the "lack of performance" of his captains on the eastbound run and insisted they do better or face unemployment and disgrace. And the Collins Line was improving. Records show that in the first eleven months of 1852, all four captains managed to beat Cunard soundly on both the eastbound and westbound voyages.

In 1852, Luce faced enormous pressure to improve his ship's time. He had achieved a great victory in February, and he intended to do all he could to better it. The Great Atlantic Race was still too close to call. Cunard was fighting back. He had added two new ships, *Asia* and

Africa, to his line. Lindsay, with his British perspective, noted, "They were sister ships but, though magnificent vessels, they were not equal in speed to those which the Collins Company had sent forth." He added, "The competition between these two great lines of steam-ships excited extraordinary public interest at the time on both sides of the Atlantic, and indeed in all parts of the world; numerous records were kept for twelve months of the length of the respective voyages of the ships of the contending companies, and large sums of money were expended in bets on the result of each passage."

Failing to match Collins with his new ships, Cunard began running his vessels twice a month during the winter, as opposed to the monthly sailings of the Collins Line in that most tempestuous of seasons. As a consequence of the expanded sailings and the greater number of ships in the Cunard fleet, the Cunarders still carried more mail than the steamers of the Collins Line. This infuriated Collins, who insisted on ever faster passages without regard to the costs. A close business associate of Cunard commented, "The Collins Company are pretty much in the situation of finding that breaking our windows with sovereigns, though very fine fun, is too costly to keep up."

Indeed, by 1852, Collins recognized that he needed a government bailout if he was to stay in business. In January, he petitioned Congress to increase its annual subsidy. The request was hotly debated, and its passage remained in doubt as Luce sailed on in that stormy sea in March. Over $3 million had been invested in the Collins Line, which had paid no dividends to stockholders. The stock was worth only fifty cents on the dollar of the original investment, and without help from the government, the company was to cease operating its ships on May 15, according to a speech by Senator William H. Seward on behalf of Collins before Congress on April 27, 1852. (Seward later became famous for his purchase of Alaska from Russia as secretary of state in 1867.)

Uncertainty, though discomforting, was no stranger to Luce. The sea had taught him that nothing remained the same for long. For the most part, he was able to suppress his anxiety and instead focus on the business at hand: running the ship and tending to his passengers. He simply had to have faith that the good men in Congress who believed in his shipowner's mission would come through with the money.

On the night of March 24, four days into the voyage, the storm's fury increased markedly. The ship labored hard in the seas that now broke over the bow. Solid water washed down the promenade deck, and it was becoming unsafe for the passengers to venture outside. The violent motion jarred the paddle wheels and made the engines run rough. Occasionally, one of the wheels lifted clear of the crests and spun rapidly with a frightful noise, before plunging deep into the top of the next wave. The masts yanked hard on the rigging supporting them. Together with Robert Gourlay, Luce surveyed the mainmast with grave concern. It seemed as though it might pull right out of the deck. Above the mainmast was another vertical spar, called a topmast. Its height above deck acted as a lever on the mainmast below, wrenching the entire length of both spars in a dangerous manner.

"Call all hands, Mister Gourlay," he said. "We'll have that main topmast housed before it comes down of its own accord."

Housing the topmast was dangerous for the crew, but the risks seemed merited. Gourlay sent for the off-watch immediately, and in a few minutes sailors gathered around the mainmast and began to prepare for the housing. They first had to remove the royal and topsail yards from the spar, send them down to the deck, and retract the topmast from its position at the doublings in order to lower it halfway down the mainmast below it. If done successfully, the maneuver reduced windage aloft and doubled up the masts for added strength.

One by one, the best sailors aboard *Arctic* ascended the ratlines as the night deepened around them. The wind howled and screamed in the rigging, taking their breath away if they turned their faces into it full on. The second officer climbed aloft as well, as was his duty, and supervised his men. About halfway through the job, the steamship plowed into an enormous wave and lurched sideways, stopping nearly dead in the water as she shouldered aside the breaking crest. John Abbott, the reporter for *Harper's*, was on deck observing the men aloft. He described what happened next:

> It was fearful to see the sailors clinging to the ropes as the ship rolled to and fro in these vast billows. Suddenly there was a loud outcry, and terrific groans came from the topmast. A poor sailor had somehow got his arm caught, and it was being crushed amidst the ponderous spars, far up in the dark and stormy sky. Oh, how drearily those groans fell upon the ear. After some time, he was extricated and helped down, and placed in the care of the surgeon.

Accidents such as these were common aboard the sailing packets and oceangoing steamers, which carried sail in the 1850s. Men risked crippling injury or death as part of their daily work, for which they received twelve dollars per month. The captain held the lives of his men in his hands, and like a general, he had to spend them on occasion for the greater good of the ship and her company. Like most other captains, Luce generally did not feel guilt or sorrow for wounded crewmen. But he had compassion. He looked in on his own in the surgery to see that the doctor had done all he could, then returned to the deck to keep watch with his officers as *Arctic* continued on her way through the storm, fighting for every mile she made good toward Liverpool at all possible speed in the Great Atlantic Race.

CHAPTER FIVE

FORTUNE OF WAR

THE INTERMITTENT RUMBLE of cannon fire filled the air in the valley of Balaklava, a narrow swath that cut into the southwestern
coast of the Crimean peninsula and led down to an insignificant harbor on the Black Sea. At the head of the valley, beyond its steep hills, a
plateau stretched out for miles. High above the harbor on the grassy
plain, the thuds and explosions of shells and the crack of muskets
became far more distinct. Pungent gray smoke drifted across the bat-
tlefield. It stung the eyes of the British troops huddled in their en-
campment thousands of miles away from their homes in England, the
comforting touch of the warm hands of their wives, and the shrill
laughter of their children.

It was strange, this corner of the world beyond the British Empire.
The Crimea was neither barren like the deserts of North Africa nor sti-
fling like the jungles of the Congo; it was a fertile land replete with pas-
ture for sheep and horses, fields of grain in the northern lowlands, and
vineyards nestled on the slopes of the humped blue and green backs of
the Crimean Mountains on the southeast coast. Surrounded on all
sides with water except the isthmus of Perekop connecting the peninsula to the mainland in what is now known as Ukraine, the Black Sea
washed against Crimea's beaches on all but the northeastern shores
fronted by the Sea of Azov and the broad expanse of the Russian empire to the east.

War, however, had begun to ravage the landscape, staining its soil
with blood as 26,000 British soldiers poured into the region, their force
nearly at maximum strength in the cool September days of 1854. They

joined the 30,000 French troops and the small contingent of 5,000 men from the Ottoman Empire gathered to lay siege to the nearby Russian naval base at Sevastopol. Among these forces was a brigade of light cavalry numbering 673 men, who would later become immortalized in Alfred, Lord Tennyson's poem "Charge of the Light Brigade" after nearly 250 died in an assault on Russian gun emplacements at Balaklava on October 25.

The war with Russia and its European neighbors to the west had been long in coming. Russia's czar, Nicholas I, wished to expand the reach of Russian influence well into central Asia east of the Caspian Sea and to the west all the way to the Aegean and Mediterranean. The Black Sea sparkled as a landlocked jewel with access to the greater world beyond available only through the narrow Bosporus strait that separates the continents of Europe and Asia. The waterway was under the control of the Ottoman Empire, which had slowly been coming apart and hovered at the brink of collapse in the decades leading up to 1854. Already the Greeks had won independence in the 1820s, and the inhabitants of the Balkans grew restless. The acquisition of the lands of the Ottoman Empire, including Turkey, and its shining city of Constantinople (present-day Istanbul), seemed possible first through diplomatic attempts to encourage Britain to join with Russia in a move against the Turks. When these and other attempts to compromise the Turks failed, Russia mobilized its army and navy and invaded Turkish lands.

The invasion triggered an almost immediate response from Great Britain and France. A British fleet had been dispatched to Besika Bay in June 1853 to defend Constantinople should the Russians attack through the Bosporus strait. With the Russian forces on the move in the Danubian Principalities of the Ottoman Empire, France and Britain joined to curb Russia's westward expansion. As a major power in the Mediterranean, Britain considered the conflict between Russia and the Ottoman Empire a direct threat to its own national security. Britain raised a small army and sent additional ships to fight against the Russian Navy. To carry troops on the long trip from England to the Crimea, the British Admiralty called on Samuel Cunard to stand by his contract and convert his liners into ships of war.

One by one through 1854, the Cunard steamships were taken out of the transatlantic trade and converted into troop transports, bringing to fruition their dual role as passenger vessels for the pleasure of travelers to practical instruments for waging war on distant battlegrounds. The Cunard steamers cruised down the Atlantic to the Straits of Gibraltar into the Mediterranean. They steamed eastward to the Aegean Sea past the Isle of Crete, up through the Sea of Marmara and the Bosporus strait to the Black Sea. Where passengers once lounged in the main saloons, soldiers prepared for battle. The holds crammed with fine freight and mail were now loaded with guns and ammunition. Horses were also transported, their whinnies and stamps an odd accompaniment to the wash of the bow wave and the slap of the paddle wheels.

By September 1854, fourteen Cunard liners were engaged in transporting troops to the carnage and death in the Crimea. This bloody little war would have far-reaching implications for England. As it dragged on and nearly 22,000 soldiers perished from malnutrition, disease, exposure to the elements, and Russian gunfire, a revolt against interventionist practices of the Crown and Parliament gained strength, but in September the casualties of the Crimean conflict remained low. The nation gallantly answered the call to action for the good of queen and country with patriotic fervor. The deployment of Cunard's liners to the Black Sea meant sacrificing the strong presence Cunard had won in the arena of commerce. The consequent strengthening of his rival, Collins, seemed a small price.

The deployment of the vast majority of Cunard's vessels for use in the war effort resulted in the termination of regular service to Boston. The Cunard docks at Jersey City remained in operation, but with the number of liners calling at New York down to a bare minimum, the activity there decreased dramatically. Much of the business went to

Collins by default, yet another bit of good luck for Collins—another reprieve from potential ruin that had appeared imminent just two years ago.

Just as he and Luce had hoped, Congress had bailed his company out. The fortunes of the Collins Line had indeed looked dim in 1852, with the company in dire financial condition and dependent on the good graces of politicians in Congress to save the enterprise and, by extension, preserve the national honor it had earned for the United States. Writing for *Harper's*, John S. C. Abbott voiced the prevailing view among the general public, one well known to the decision makers in Washington and shared by many of them:

> The United States have never yet done anything which has contributed as much to their honor in Europe, as the construction of this Collins line of steamers. We have made a step in advance of the whole world. Nothing ever before floated equal to these ships. Their speed is in accordance with their magnificence. No one thinks of questioning their superiority. Every American abroad feels personally ennobled by them, and participates in his country's glory. . . . It is not to be supposed that such ships should be immediately profitable to the owners. They were built for national glory. They do exalt and honor our nation. How much more glorious is such a triumph of humanity and art, than any celebrity attained by the horrors and the misery of war. The English government liberally patronizes the Cunard line of steamers. This line [Collins] now needs the patronage of the government of the United States. We had far better sink half a dozen of our ships of war, important as they may be, than allow these ships to be withdrawn.

Aware of the public support he enjoyed, Edward Knight Collins was far from admitting defeat or that the ostentatious way in which he operated the steamships was unnecessary. He conducted an expert lobbying campaign designed to win the hearts of the congressmen he needed to get behind the increase in the government subsidy. He sent *Baltic* up the Potomac River to show the politicians of sleepy Washington, D.C., just what kind of ships he had sent forth to combat Samuel Cunard. Many of the elected officials had not seen a Collins steamer before, much less enjoyed the fine dining and freely flowing liquor that made these ships famous from New York to Liverpool. President Millard Fillmore, members of his cabinet, and any politician privileged to move in the right circles rode steamboats from Washington to *Baltic*'s anchorage. Suitably impressed, members of Congress voted in favor of increasing the annual subsidy of $385,000 to $858,000, and the line was saved. The Collins Line matched Cunard's winter voyages, evening the competition with a total of twenty-six round-trip crossings every year.

Even with the added funds from the U.S. Treasury, the company ran in the red all through 1853. The solvency of the line was constantly in question, and congressmen began to reconsider whether it was worth continuing to support a line of ships that might or might not be needed in case of war. Detractors contended that it made more sense to let the British carry the U.S. mail because it would cost half as much as it did with the Collins Line. When Britain found itself at war with Russia, the value of the steamships soon became apparent, and the controversy surrounding Collins and his steamships died down for a while. Early in 1854, it seemed to many that dogged determination and the effects of the Crimean War had made Collins the unchallenged master of the western ocean.

ACROSS THE NORTH RIVER IN MANHATTAN, the Collins docks hummed in late summer with throngs of passengers, wagons delivering freight and mail, and well-wishers present to see their loved ones off. Mere spectators ambled down to the waterfront to witness the departure of these fleetest of vessels. Ship watching had become something of a citywide pastime, and there was plenty to observe. The clipper ships of New York engaged in the California trade lined the East River, sharing dockage space with the packets in the transatlantic service. On April 20, 1854, the clipper ship *Flying Cloud* had broken her own record for the fastest passage on the 16,000-mile run from New York to San Francisco, making the journey around Cape Horn in only eighty-nine days, eight hours. She made headlines on both sides of the Atlantic and stoked American national pride, already approaching irrational levels.

Out in the harbor, the sleek yachts of the New York Yacht Club raced to the cheers of crowds lining the shores to witness the frequent regattas. Yacht *America*, which sailed under the flag of the New York Yacht Club to victory in a race around the Isle of Wight in 1851, was famous among New Yorkers. The New York Yacht Club took home a trophy worth one hundred pounds; it later became known as the America's Cup, the prize in match races today that still rivet yachting enthusiasts throughout the world. Never before had the United States been in a more enviable position in terms of prowess on the high seas, and New York, the economic and cultural capital of the nation, stood at the center of it all.

The usual confusion and frenetic pace reigned at the foot of Canal Street as Captain Luce supervised the preparations for his latest trip across the Atlantic Ocean in early September. He welcomed the more important first-class passengers aboard. Standing off out of the way were his manservant, Abraham Boydell, and his son, Willie, now age eleven and still in poor health.

Willie's condition made it impossible for him to lead the life of a normal boy his age, and both his parents had decided to take him out of school for a short time to enjoy the adventure of a sea voyage aboard *Arctic*. Based on the boy's enthusiastic response to the news that he would travel with his father and see the sights of Liverpool, the decision to bring him along seemed right and pleased his mother, Elizabeth. Luce, too, was happy to have Willie accompany him on the voyage. His duties as *Arctic*'s master occupied most of his time, and he had little left to share with his family. Robert, a young man of eighteen, was due to attend Rensselaer Polytechnic Institute in Troy, New York, on September 27. He was already carving out a niche for himself, making his own way in life to pursue his ambition to become an engineer, leaving only Willie at home. The voyage provided Luce with a rare opportunity for extended contact with Willie, and he, like his son, had looked forward to this particular round-trip crossing with more than the usual routine anticipation that comes with the prospect of a passage across the North Atlantic on the eve of the arrival of the gales of winter.

Leaning against Boydell for support, Willie proudly watched his father at work, an important man dashing in appearance in his fine clothes, his cap perched at an angle on his crown of thick brown hair, the quick smile he gave to each of the passengers as they greeted him warmly. Many of them had sailed on *Arctic* before and knew Luce well, both for his skills as a navigator and his ability to entertain them at the captain's table. For Willie, the ritual of embarkation seemed magical, the moment an exciting start to an adventure.

By early afternoon, *Arctic* was ready to set sail. The pilot came aboard, and Luce ordered Robert Gourlay to cast off the ship's warps and back her out of her berth. The reports from the signal cannon no doubt delighted young boys like Willie. He would have cheered with the rest of the passengers as the paddle wheels churned the water white and the vessel began to move, slowly at first, before picking up speed on her way down the upper bay to the open ocean beyond Sandy Hook. Seamen scurried about making sail. They inched out along the footropes suspended beneath the yards, untied the gaskets holding the sails securely to the spars, and quickly descended the ratlines back to the deck. Each man moved in tandem with his mate in a strange kind of dance. Deckhands strained and swayed as they heaved on the halyards to raise the heavy yards, singing out a chantey to keep the coordinated rhythm of their work. Their gruff voices contrasted against the more refined talk of the passengers. Slowly the yards rose up the mast, and wind filled the canvas.

Like most other young boys on their first adventure at sea, no doubt Willie would have wanted to stay on deck with the rest of the people to watch the hills of the Highlands of Navesink grow more distinct the closer the ship came to the end of the Main Ship Channel and the immediate environs of Sandy Hook bar. The pale green, yellow, and orange foliage of the approaching fall set the hills on shore above the white sands of the beaches aglow in colors that would grow more pronounced as the season progressed. It was a beautiful sight, one that inspired comments from passengers and drove home the point that soon the empty reaches of the sea would surround them until the craggy heights of the Irish coast hove into view at the end of the voyage.

Out past Romer Shoal and the North Beacon at the tip of Sandy Hook, *Arctic* steadily and swiftly steamed. The narrow channel past the sand spit took her close to the surf breaking on the beach. Gulls wheeled above the ship. A blue flag emblazoned in gold with an eagle and shield, the seal of the United States, fluttered and snapped from the top of the main topmast, indicating that she carried mail for the government. The Stars and Stripes flew from a tall varnished staff at the stern. A long wake trailed behind the vessel where the disturbed water met and smoothed the tidal chop with a slick.

The pilot ordered *Arctic* put a point or two to starboard as she made the easy turn into the last stretch of Gedney Channel out over the shoals that created a natural barrier across most of the lower bay. Off to port, the Sandy Hook Lightship rode bow to the swells of the Atlantic, her powerful lamp affixed to a globe at the main masthead. She lay four miles to the east and represented the last of the aids to navigation at the approaches to New York Harbor. Once clear of the bar, the pilot turned to Luce and smiled.

"We're well away from any danger, Captain," he said, the wind whipping his hair, his face calm with the experience of years under sail in the fast schooners that carried him far out to sea in search of ships to guide home to safety. He pointed to a nearby schooner and nodded, indicating he wanted to be put off the steamer.

"Very good," Luce replied. He leaned over the rails of the paddle-wheel box and shouted to Robert Gourlay. "Bring her hard up on the wind, Mister Gourlay. All ahead slow."

Gourlay acknowledged the orders. He tugged the bell pull that led to the wheelhouse far astern, giving it two quick yanks. Back in the wheelhouse, the helmsman responded by turning the wheel slightly to the right, then checked the turn when the bell rang out signaling him to stop. *Arctic*'s bow came up until the wind blew nearly from ahead, just far enough off to keep the wind in most of the sails. Under command of Second Mate William Baalham, sailors on deck manned the sheets and braces of the square sails, and backed the main topsail while others sheeted home the spencers. At the same time, Gourlay signaled chief engineer J. W. Rogers in the engine room to reduce power. The number of revolutions the paddle wheels made per minute dropped from their average of fifteen to barely enough to keep the ship head to the wind.

As the passengers watched, a small rowboat was lowered from the schooner, her sails luffing in the breeze, the way almost off her. In minutes, the younger members of the pilot boat's crew, apprentices in training under their more experienced mates, rowed across to the steamship. The pilot said good-bye to Luce, wishing him a safe and speedy crossing. He climbed over the bulwarks of the main deck abaft the paddle wheel and descended down the clifflike side of the ship to the boat nearly two stories below.

Luce waited until the boat had fallen astern. "We'll fill away now, Mister Gourlay. All ahead full."

"Aye, Captain. Fill away and all ahead full!"

Almost simultaneously, the teamwork needed to get *Arctic* back

under full power began. Sailors on deck hauled hard on the main topsail braces as the ship turned onto her easterly course, bringing the
wind abeam. The main topsail filled with a pleasing boom and drew
hard in the fresh breeze. Other sailors eased the spencer sheets for a
broad reach, letting the massive booms and gaffs fall off at a slight
angle to leeward for the best aerodynamic lift from the sails.

Arctic came round to her proper heading just as the men below in
the engine room brought the powerful machines up to speed. The paddle wheels beat the swells faster and faster. The coal heavers hastened
the pace of their never-ending cycle of shoveling coal from the bunkers
to feed the furnaces beneath the steamer's four boilers. The oilers
moved about with cans of oil and squirted the lubricant where it was
needed. Engineers monitored the steam pressure, checked the bearings to ensure they did not run hot, and completed a multitude of
other tiny tasks. Firemen tended the furnaces, their faces streaked
with sweat and blackened with coal dust and soot. Above deck, the evidence of their work rose as acrid black smoke up the seventy-five-foot-
tall funnel and blew off to starboard to the south, a stark contrast
against the white sails and the shimmering blue of the waves.

The ship safely on her way, Luce had one more important duty to
attend prior to turning the watch over to Gourlay. He waved to Willie
as he hurried past him to the chart house, where he grabbed a hand
bearing compass. He returned to the top of the paddle-wheel box and
took a bearing on the lightship, on Sandy Hook Light, and the twin
lights on the summit of Navesink's steep slopes. He returned to the
chart house and plotted the lines of position he had obtained with the
bearings. The intersection of the lines on the chart indicated *Arctic*'s
precise position. He noted this plot in the log as his official point of departure. It would be the first of many fixes, but the last based on terrestrial objects until the ship made landfall in approximately ten days.

His duty done for the moment, he strode briskly back to the
paddle-wheel box and gave Gourlay the con. It was the custom for the
first officer to take the first watch when leaving port, and Luce liked to

execute his duty in a traditional way. At the height of his powers as a mariner, he exuded the confidence that comes from a career as successful as his, the recognition he had received in his tenure aboard the packets of the Red Star Line and subsequently with Collins. As was the case on most merchant vessels except in bad weather, Luce kept all hands in the sailing department at work from early morning until four o'clock. After that, the deck crew stood what was known as watch and watch, meaning they served in shifts of four hours on and four hours off. William Baalham, the second officer, would take the port watch when it was time to relieve Gourlay.

The men responsible for running the engines occupied a world alien to that of the sailors working the sails on deck, and they were seldom seen by the passengers. The black gang answered to J. W. Rogers and his corps of officers. Luce did not have much to do with them, except that as captain he represented the ultimate authority aboard the vessel. He bore the sole responsibility for the ship's safety and her success or failure. In many ways, he was like a god. Few other men outside the military shared such power.

Gourlay took his station on the paddle-wheel box and kept a weather eye on the heavy traffic moving all around the steamer. Fishing boats, coastal schooners, steam ferries, an occasional yacht or two, sailing packets, and clippers filled the sea. Vigilance was required at all times when departing from the busiest port in the United States. Collisions in fog and storms occurred with alarming frequency. Duty aboard the pilot boats and aboard the Sandy Hook Lightship was dangerous due to the increasing number of ships calling at New York. It was less dangerous for the massive steamships. They tended to run down and crush the smaller craft in the event of accidents. That fact was widely acknowledged.

Captain Luce descended from his perch on the paddle-wheel box and joined Boydell and Willie on deck. The cool wind blowing off the port beam tinged the boy's cheeks into rosy patches. Luce noticed he shivered but allowed him to stay on deck. He spent much of his life at home in his bed. It was a special experience for him to be so much a part of the action. He looked animated now.

All around him, Willie would have seen male passengers dressed in their fine dark suits, topcoats, and black high hats. The ladies with full skirts and slender waists were there on deck too, with their coats and shawls, and hats pulled tight against the chilly breeze. In obvious view were the four lifeboats suspended on davits on deck behind the paddle wheels. Two other boats were stored forward on top of the deckhouses. At only thirty feet or so in length, they were ridiculously small compared to the enormity of *Arctic*. But no one minded that as they observed the land receding astern, the busy approaches to the biggest city in America, a thriving metropolis the graceful steamship would never reach again.

CHAPTER SIX

PORTENT

A T SEA, THE CEASELESS MOTION, the salt in the air, and the relent-less ocean swells transport one's sense of identity, some say to the sublime. But most sailors admit to a pleasure in seeing any such sublimity come to a stop. As *Arctic* approached Cape Clear on the southern coast of Ireland on September 12, 1854, the ship's company looked forward to reaching shore. At noon, the passengers gathered for their daily update of the ship's position. They were anxious to know how close they were to the adventures to begin when the ship rested alongside the quay at her port of call.

On an earlier voyage aboard *Arctic*, John S. C. Abbott described these emotions:

> The captain informed us that we were 95 miles from Cape Clear at noon to-day, and that we might expect to see the coast of Ireland about six o'clock. The day has been magnificently beautiful. We have seen many ships in the horizon, indicating that we were leaving the solitudes of the ocean behind us. Immediately after dinner all the passengers assembled upon deck to catch the first glimpse of land. At just a quarter before six o'clock [Captain Luce's dead reckoning was spot on] we saw the highlands of the Irish coast looming through the haze before us.
>
> No one who has not crossed the ocean can conceive of the joyous excitement of the scene. All the discomfort of ocean life was forgotten in the exhilaration of the hour. As twilight

faded away, the outline of the shore became more visible under the rays of a most brilliant moon. Soon the light from Cape Clear beamed brilliantly before us. . . . We are rapidly sailing up the channel, having still some two hundred and fifty miles to make, before we land in Liverpool. But our ocean life is ended. We have crossed the Atlantic.

Arctic rounded the southern tip of Ireland and joined the parade of shipping proceeding up and down St. George Channel into the Irish Sea, an often tempestuous, tide-driven waterway between the islands comprising England and Scotland, and Ireland. She steamed off Liverpool Bay by early September 13 and under the careful guidance of a pilot slowly made her way across the sandbars at the mouth of the Mersey River estuary on a rising tide.

Like New York, the thriving port of Liverpool had its natural barriers to shipping. Despite constant efforts of the steam dredges, the depth at the river mouth was just eleven feet at low water during the lowest tides. Fully loaded, *Arctic* drew nineteen feet, requiring the aid of the tide to get her safely across the bar. However, in the waters of the Mersey River, the tide rose and fell thirty-one feet during the highest tides, accounting for the ability of the largest ships to call at the port, the busiest in the world. It surpassed New York, Boston, New Orleans, Halifax, Le Havre, Bremen, and burgeoning Hamburg.

The docks of Liverpool stretched along the eastern shore of the river for more than five miles, and every year more work was done to improve and expand the port facilities. Situated in northwestern England near the major manufacturing center of Manchester, Liverpool had long since outstripped Portsmouth, Southampton, and Bristol in terms of its economic importance and the number of vessels calling there. The evidence of its bustling activity became clear to the passengers lining the rails of *Arctic*'s promenade deck. Steamboats, barges, cutters, dredges, coastal traders, packets, clippers, and steamships from England, France, Germany, and the United States seemed to occupy every square inch of space in mid-channel, and the berths set behind the massive sea walls. The tips of masts protruded above the barriers like a forest.

W. S. Lindsay wrote proudly of Liverpool in the 1870s:

Liverpool, including Birkenhead, has a far larger amount of dock accommodation than any other port in Great Britain, or, indeed, in the world, and no works of a similar character, of ancient or modern times, can be compared with them. . . . The docks themselves are the marvel of the place. Along the whole of the eastern bank of the river (the site of Liverpool) there will shortly be for upwards of six miles in length, the finest network of wet-docks in the world, protected by a sea wall of an average thickness of eleven feet, and forty feet in height from its foundations, faced with massive blocks of granite, perhaps in itself one of the greatest works of the kind of modern times. . . . Nearly all the docks are surrounded with open sheds on the quays for the reception and temporary stowage of goods and produce. Many of these are handsome structures and all of them substantial and very commodious.

Along the shores beyond the waterfront, hotels, shops, taverns, and boardinghouses clustered on the narrow, dirty streets. It was a tough town full of sailors, longshoremen, crimps, and thieves. Thousands of immigrants crowded the streets on any given day. The port was both an industrial complex and a staging area for the mass exodus of the disenfranchised fleeing the poverty and political unrest that in recent times had struck Britain, Ireland, Germany, Scandinavia, and France. Between 1815 and 1854, 4.1 million immigrants left the United Kingdom bound for the United States of America, and of that number 1.3 million departed between 1850 and 1854. Most of them filtered through Liverpool.

The heavy traffic on the river kept Luce and his officers alert for any potential danger as they nudged *Arctic* into her berth at Huskisson Dock, one of the largest in Liverpool. When she came to rest, Luce shouted a series of orders for Gourlay, Baalham, Third Mate Francis Dorian, and the other officers under his command to carry out. Sailors set to securing the ship for her week at the dock, making cables fast, coiling lines, and laying aloft to tightly furl the square sails and brail in the fore and main spencers. The yards they adjusted to sit exactly perpendicular to the hull, squared in Bristol fashion, as the sailors called it.

Upon receiving word from the captain, Chief Engineer J. W. Rogers and his assistants blew off steam to reduce the pressure in the boilers. The coal heavers and firemen stopped their work, wiped the grime from their faces, and anticipated the carnal delights that awaited them on shore in the brothels that proliferated in Liverpool's red light district. But the more skilled members of the black gang would have little time for the shoreside pleasures typical of a seaman. Their duty required them to stay below and work on the engines, always in need of servicing after running full out over 3,000 miles of open ocean.

Up on deck, a controlled chaos ensued among the passengers. Stewards dashed about helping them gather their belongings in the main saloon, ready for the mandatory close inspection from the customs officials. This could take hours, and many of the men sought refuge at the bar to pass the time, keeping the bartenders and waiters as busy as ever. Once the luggage was cleared, porters trundled the bags and trunks down the gangway to the wharf and loaded them onto horse-drawn taxis waiting to take the travelers to their lodgings for the night or to meet one of the trains leaving Liverpool for points east.

By the next day, *Arctic* was virtually deserted. Only her crew remained aboard, cleaning, painting, reprovisioning, and working aloft on the rigging, tarring the stays and shrouds, and taking up the slack where necessary. Coalers came alongside, and much of the black gang was seen on deck transferring tons of it from the barges to replenish the nearly empty bunkers. J. W. Rogers kept his engineers hard at work as well.

A native of New London, Connecticut, Rogers was a hardened veteran of the sea, like so many of the other Yankee sailors who hailed from that bustling port on eastern Long Island Sound. Unlike his peers serving aboard sailing ships, however, he had spent most of his life aboard steam vessels in the coastal trade and on the rivers and sounds of the Northeast and South. He was among the best of his profession, in part due to his acquisition of invaluable knowledge regarding marine steam engines from his father, Moses. He and his brothers grew up admiring and emulating Moses. He was, in fact, something of a legend.

Back in 1809, Colonel John Stevens, one of the richest men in New Jersey, who had been a pioneer in steam transportation on land and sea, entrusted Moses with his 100-foot steamboat *Phoenix* on the first ocean voyage ever made under steam power alone. He set out from the safety of the upper bay of New York, steamed down past Sandy Hook, and headed south along the treacherous New Jersey coast to Delaware Bay. Blocked by a monopoly on ferry service on the North River, which had begun when Robert Fulton and his backers sent the steamboat *Clermont* (the vessel also used sails on occasion) from New York to Albany in 1807, Stevens determined to establish his own monopoly on the Delaware. *Phoenix* served as a vital link in a land and river service between New York and Philadelphia for many years and augmented the Stevens fortune.

Moses Rogers was one of the first American masters fully to appreciate the role steam might play in the merchant marine. Convinced that transatlantic steamship voyages were possible, he petitioned wealthy New York merchants for financial backing to test his theory just about the time the men behind the Black Ball Line hatched their scheme to launch regular packet service. The would-be backers laughed at the insanity of the idea, just as they had laughed at John Stevens when he suggested, also around the same time, that railroads, as opposed to the Erie Canal, were the way of the future for transporting goods into the interior. Undaunted, Moses went South for backing. He found a more sanguine welcome from merchants in the cotton port of Savannah, Georgia. A group of these foresighted southerners paid for the construction of the 380-ton full-rigged ship *Savannah* and had her outfitted with steam engines and retractable paddle wheels.

On May 24, 1819, Moses set sail from Savannah bound for Liverpool. His ship made the passage in twenty-seven days, according to noted marine historian Robert Greenhalgh Albion in his book *The Rise of New York Port*. Moses's exploit received much attention in the press. Although he had used sail for most of the voyage, deploying his paddle wheels and firing up the steam engines only when it was calm and taking the whole rig inboard when it was not, he proved that a steam-powered vessel could be used on a crossing of the western ocean. The rise of the New York packets at exactly the same time helped steer the merchants and shipowners away from the pursuit of steam, until advances in Great Britain forced them to follow suit.

It was in part because of his father's fame that Collins sought out J. W. Rogers as one of his best engineers. The son was known to have his father's knack with engines. J. W. Rogers served first aboard *Atlantic*, meticulously nursing her engines for three years, until 1853. He was then posted to Luce's command aboard *Arctic*. There was a reason for the timing of the change. Considered at the top of his profession, Rogers was transferred to work on an important upgrade to the steamer's machinery.

Arctic was to be the first of the Collins liners to have the benefits of a "super-heating apparatus," as it was called. The device increased the temperature of the steam inside the boilers, slowing condensation and consequently making better use of the steam to drive the engines more efficiently. Installed in August 1854, it marked one of the first times such an apparatus was used in an oceangoing liner. Rogers was constantly checking it in those first weeks of its service aboard *Arctic* to make certain it functioned according to specifications.

As the ship lay to her berth, Rogers and his six officers and other skilled workers set about overhauling the engines for the return trip to New York. Because she drew seawater directly into her boilers to make steam, the buildup of salt and rust from corrosion presented a persistent maintenance challenge. The boilers contained more than five thousand tubes that clogged with debris or simply wore out from the nearly constant exposure to the heat and water. The disadvantages of evaporating seawater were well known. Collins intended to outfit each of his steamers with the very latest advances in marine steam engine technology to allow for the evaporation of fresh water in the boilers.

Writing in his book *Naval and Mail Steamers of the United States* in 1853, Charles B. Stuart, engineer-in-chief of the U.S. Navy, pointed out Collins's best efforts to secure the most up-to-date machinery for his ships and the twist of fate that thwarted him:

> It was the original intention of Mr. Collins . . . to use fresh water entirely in these boilers, previously condensed from sea water, and an arrangement was accordingly made with J. P. Pirsson, inventor of the "Double Vacuum Condenser," to furnish condensers for this purpose. Orders for the tubes were sent out to England, but in consequence of their loss at sea . . . the vessels of the line were equipped without them. It is to be regretted, that circumstances should have prevented the introduction of this important element of additional economy and success, and the author is informed by Mr. Collins, that it is his intention in fitting out the next steamer of the line, to avail himself of the advantages involved in the evaporation of fresh water.

The engineers on *Arctic* and the other Collins ships worked with the older technology and did the best they could to avoid breakdowns. Rogers and his immediate subordinate, First Assistant Engineer John Degnon, supervised the cleaning of the boilers and replacement of tubes where required. They checked and lubricated as needed the crossheads, crosstails, side rods, side-lever beams, connecting rods, crankshafts, valves, bearings, air pumps, feed pumps, and injectors.

For most of the men, the work was a routine matter with little in it worthy of fascination. However, for Stewart Holland, a twenty-two-year-old apprentice engineer from Washington, D.C., the complex engines were new to him, and he had much to learn. As a consequence, he pursued his duties below as if he were in the pristine lecture halls of Harvard. He believed steam represented the future in the merchant marine and that the growing nation would need an increasing number of men skilled in the workings of engines. He also believed that a man unafraid to get his hands dirty to acquire these skills would do well in the world. His mother had died when he was at an early age. His aunt, Kitty Barrett, raised him as if he was her own little boy. Holland's father, assistant sergeant-at-arms for the U.S. Senate, loved his only child dearly. He had instilled in him a sense of honor and a sense of the importance of embracing the advantages of modern life.

Holland was an unusual young man. Most of his peers still believed that the sailing ships might retain their importance and glory. The swift passages of the clipper ships seemed to prove the assertion that the "smoke boxes" must keep to their place—that they had no business traveling the globe in the interest of commerce. The clippers, in fact, did outperform the steamers of the early 1850s, sailing faster than even a Collins liner could manage at full power with a following breeze. Yet Holland, with the wisdom of youth, understood that the world was changing fast, and he wanted to be a part of the new ways, not the old ones.

It seemed magical to Holland: the hot fires of the furnaces turned the seawater inside the boilers into steam, which expanded to many times the volume of the evaporated water, creating the energy needed to drive the pistons back and forth in the cylinders, and that motion was harnessed to turn the ship's paddle wheels through the surface of the sea. Holland listened carefully to John Degnon, the gruff but kindly man who took Holland under his wing and kept the toughest of the black gang from hazing him. Holland dreamed of climbing the ranks from third junior assistant and becoming a chief engineer himself one day.

While the ship was made ready for her return voyage to New York, Luce found himself much engrossed in the business at hand. He supervised the discharging of the cargo of cotton from the South, most of which passed through New York and enriched the merchants of the big city nearly as much as it did the plantation owners. *Arctic* also brought grain from the Midwest and oil from the whaling towns of New England. These commodities represented the bulk of exports from the United States at the time. A large sum of money, in specie, was taken from the liner's vault and brought ashore under armed guard. The *Illustrated London News* noted on September 16 that the total value of specie exported from New York during 1854 thus far amounted to £5,957,480 sterling. The Collins liners carried more than just passengers and mail; the transportation of silver and gold made them an important part of international banking.

A notice in the *Herald* dated February 8, 1852, revealed just how much specie *Arctic* carried on an average voyage: "The steamer Arctic, which sailed for Liverpool yesterday afternoon, took out $925,000 in American gold, $100,000 in American silver, 2,073 pounds in British gold, and 463 pounds in British silver. Rather a valuable freight, that."

As soon as the cargo was discharged, convoys of wagons laden with expensive manufactured goods from England's factories arrived on the quay. England's main export was textiles made from the raw cotton imported from the United States. Ready-made clothing was soaring in popularity among the middle class in American cities and towns. The convenience of purchasing a garment, as opposed to making it, improved the quality of life for the woman of the house. Cookware, glassware, and other luxury items were loaded aboard. The total value of the freight was $1 million.

Men covered the steamer's decks like insects as they lowered crates and casks into the hold using the ship's main yard as a derrick. Sorting through voluminous amounts of paperwork occupied Luce's days. Sometimes it seemed to both Luce and other masters that the price paid for the most elite of commands demanded nothing more than being a good clerk. Luce nevertheless made time to take Willie ashore to explore Liverpool. They dined together at the more respectable establishments, and Luce introduced his son to some of the merchants and captains of the town, making him the center of attention—to Willie's delight.

After going over the return voyage passenger list yet again the night before their departure, Luce told Willie that they would have the pleasure of sailing with Maria Miller Brown, or Millie, as she was known. She was a friend of the family and a daughter of James Brown, president of the Collins Line, as well as the best friend of Luce's niece, Amy Fearing. Attractive, with soft features, striking dark eyes, and long brown hair, Millie was one of the most pleasant young ladies the captain knew. The fact that she took a special liking to his son further endeared her to Luce.

Luce had received word from Millie's sister, Grace, also booked for the passage, that the day of their departure was Millie's twenty-first birthday. A party was planned for dinner, which Luce arranged with the head cook and waiter. The steamer would be well on her way by three o'clock Wednesday afternoon. The festivities would provide a cheerful start for the trip across the Atlantic. Among the others on the guest list were additional members of James Brown's family and the wife and two children of Edward Knight Collins himself. This was a larger than usual number of important individuals.

The height of the travel season in Europe was drawing to its end. The winter gales of the North Atlantic had already begun to buffet the coast with strong west winds that cut through sailors' heavy wool pea coats. Those wishing to return to the United States before the worst of the storms arose hurried to the Liverpool piers to catch a fast Collins steamer bound for home, and *Arctic* was booked to capacity. With all two hundred beds in first class and many of the eighty beds in the second-class cabins taken, Luce had to fill out the crew with additional waiters, stewards, and housekeeping staff.

Luce tucked Willie into bed on the night of September 19, kissed him goodnight, and went out on deck to spend a few moments alone. He could see his breath in the cool evening air and hoped for a swift passage.

LATER THAT NIGHT, while much of Liverpool slept, a woman tossed and turned in her sleep, alone in her room in an inn catering to upper-class travelers. Despite the cold, sweat soaked her sheets and blankets. She was a middle-aged lady, the sister of a cotton merchant from Charleston, South Carolina, and had accompanied her brother, Charles Mitchell, to England for pleasure while he combined a bit of business with the trip to make it pay.

Mitchell was a big fellow with somewhat unruly jet black hair, muttonchop sideburns, and a thick mustache. A southern gentleman with a hint of granite in his personality that did him good in the count-inghouse, at age thirty-eight he enjoyed the prosperity that hard work and a good sense of the cotton trade had earned him over the years. As the market dipped and rose, he played with every bit as much savvy as the stockbrokers on Wall Street played the numbers game at the exchange. The trip abroad was a present to her, a gift of brotherly love to take her away for a time from her life as a spinster. The adventures in the Old World remained fresh in her memory. She intended to talk much about her grand expedition with her lady friends over tea when she arrived home after crossing the Atlantic aboard *Arctic*.

Suddenly she awoke with a start, the kind of abrupt jolt to consciousness that sometimes came when drifting off to sleep. She had had a nightmare, a portent of evil she did not quite understand and yet felt as a palpable presence in the room. Its meaning lingered beyond her grasp no matter how hard she concentrated and tried to identify the cause of her distress. She gripped her blankets under her chin. Her lips quivered, and a bitter taste filled her mouth. Her heart beat fast, and sleep eluded her for most of the night. The next morning, she told her brother about her dream and said she refused to set sail aboard the steamer, though she could not explain why. She had foreseen something sinister, nothing more or less, and she wanted no part of it.

"We can sail on the *Baltic*," she said. "You mustn't go."

"Nonsense, Caroline," he told her with a laugh. "I have business to attend to." He tried to convince her to come with him as planned and told her that her fears were irrational, even silly.

As hard as it was for Caroline, she still refused to go. Standing on the dock as the passengers filed up *Arctic's* gangway, she wept, feeling helpless and emptier inside than she ever had before. She spotted Charles on deck, looking down at her and smiling. He waved to her. Then the crowd closed in on him, and he disappeared.

CHAPTER SEVEN

UNWITTING PASSENGERS

A RCTIC EMERGED from the sheltered waters of the Mersey River into the wide expanse of Liverpool Bay shortly after eleven o'clock on Wednesday morning, September 20, and headed due west in the direction of Dublin on the Irish coast. Short, steep seas topped with white crests met her bow and crashed harmlessly against her hull. The ship was so large that the waves imparted only a subtle pitch, while the steam tender accompanying her to see she made it safely past the last of the shoals plunged wildly against them. Sheets of spray flew back over the tender's forecastle and wet the decks, chilling her crewmen in spite of their heavy clothing. As the eastern shore receded astern, the little steam tug turned back to port, leaving *Arctic* alone on the windswept waters of the Irish Sea.

Luce left the watch to Robert Gourlay and went aft to the chart house. The air inside was warm from the steam radiator. It was comforting, the heat, and it reminded him of home. He missed Elizabeth more than usual. Perhaps it was because she would be alone in the house in just a week, when Robert left home to start his first year in college many miles from Yonkers. He wished he could be there with her as he stared out the window of the chart house at the leaden sea and sky, the gray rocky coast of northwestern England close aboard off the port beam.

Luce sighed. The melancholy mood had no place aboard a ship filled with people celebrating all that was good in life—their fortunes and futures, the safety and security of financial privilege. Personal feelings were not allowed to surface when it came to the master. He was a host and must play his role well. Pushing away his emotions, Luce hunched over the chart and ran a few calculations. It was roughly sixty miles to Camel Head, a promontory that jutted out into the Irish Sea. This and the headland of Anglesey he must round before putting *Arctic* on a southwesterly course for Camsore Point on the midcoast of Ireland. At the ship's current speed, she would pass Camel Head at around three o'clock, just about the time the Browns and the Collinses planned to meet him and Willie in the dining saloon for Millie's party. It was another ninety miles or so from Camel Head to Camsore Point, which meant it would be dark before the ship reached it and turned to a more westerly heading to skirt the shores of the coast all the way to Cape Clear and the open ocean beyond.

Passengers began to fill the dining saloon shortly before the dinner hour. It was a "large, airy, beautiful room . . . with windows opening upon the ocean as pleasantly as those of any parlor," Abbott wrote during his passage aboard *Arctic*. For some, the stress of locating their luggage amid all the trunks and bags lined up in rows in the main saloon, and with the help of the stewards transporting it to their staterooms, the motion of the ship, however slight, and the new surroundings, regardless of their splendor, dampened their appetites. Others sat down to the tables hungry for the feasts routinely served aboard Collins liners.

Below decks in the enormous icehouse were boxes and crates loaded with all kinds of perishable foods. The typical dinner menu included a wide variety of choices. Boiled ham, turkey, and mutton with oyster, parsley, and caper sauces, baked stuffed cod, roast beef, veal, lamb, duck, and pork composed the main courses. *Macaroni au gratin, filet de pigeon au cronstaught, salmis de canard sauvage, fricandeau de tortue au petit pois*, and other specialty entrees were also served.

Diners rounded out their repasts with desserts such as almond cup custards; red currant, cranberry, and apple tarts; Coventry puffs; vermicelli pudding; and other delicacies made fresh in the galley under the supervision of the ship's pastry chef. Preparing these meals kept nine cooks and additional assistants working full time. Passengers aboard Collins ships wanted speed, but they also expected to dine as well as they might at Delmonico's, one of the most fashionable restaurants in New York City.

Captain Luce returned to the deck and took his post beside Robert Gourlay atop the paddle-wheel box, his face to the stiff cold westerly breeze. The wind tousled his hair along the sides of his cap, and his eyes watered a little from the salt lifted from the waves into the air. Below him, the immense wheel churned as it dug into the waves, pushing up a mound of dark water forward and raining solid water aft that left a band of white foam to run along the side of the hull back toward the stern. He drew his gold watch from his vest pocket and checked the time. He was aware of the passengers on deck gathering at the doors of the dining saloon. He did not wish to be late for his special guests, no doubt already at the captain's table. But he had his duty to see to his ship first.

He raised his leather-bound spyglass and squinted into the lens. Fine off the port bow, Camel Head loomed above the sea. It was a desolate finger of rock nearly at the extreme western edge of England in those waters. He lowered the glass and prepared to determine the steamer's distance from land, as well as her exact position in relation to the shoals in the vicinity.

Luce took a series of bearings on terrestrial objects ashore—lighthouses, daymarks, prominent buildings—that coincided with those indicated on his chart, and he jotted down the figures in a notebook. He asked Gourlay to assist him as he used his sextant to measure the height of the headland from the surface of the water, taking into account his own elevation off the sea high up on *Arctic*'s paddle-wheel box, as well as the height of the tide at that hour. This information he used to calculate distance off. It was not an exceptionally complex undertaking, merely a necessary routine. The currents ran swiftly around headlands, and they could set *Arctic* off her intended course. The promontories also funneled wind into blasts and regularly kicked up a nasty sea, especially in autumn and winter. No wise navigator took rounding an imposing point lightly. To do so invited trouble.

Luce returned to the chart house and plotted *Arctic*'s position, then went back on deck. Satisfied she was safe for the moment, he told Gourlay to call Baalham's watch. "Set fore staysail, the jib, and fore and main spencers when we round the point, Mister Gourlay. She'll carry those well, though I think we'll be pinched too tight for the square-sails."

Luce looked out at Camel Head, now coming almost abeam with the steamer speeding through the waves at thirteen knots. He climbed down the stairs on the paddle-wheel box to the deck and went to Willie's cabin to get the boy. Inside the expansive stateroom, he found Abraham Boydell and his son talking and laughing together. Boydell was a good man, more a devoted friend of the Luce family than a hired servant, and he had formed a tight bond with Willie. In a sense, he was almost like a substitute father when Luce was away, a thought that both delighted and hurt Luce.

"We're off now, as soon as you're ready," Luce said.

Boydell helped Willie dress for dinner and said he hoped he would have a good time.

The mildly discordant hum of conversations—most in English but others in French, German, and Italian—the clink of dishes, and the scurry of the waiters filled the dining saloon. Some of the passengers interrupted their talk and glanced in Luce's direction, whispering, "Look, there's the captain!" Some wondered what was wrong with the little boy with him, why he limped so badly. The men who already knew Luce stood up to shake his hand as he passed.

At the captain's table, the guests of honor welcomed Luce like the old friend he was, as he made Willie comfortable in the seat next to his. Before he sat down himself, he greeted each person. He started with Mary Ann Collins, the pretty though somewhat eccentric wife of

Edward Knight Collins. She was a deep believer in spiritualism. She swore that she and Edward were able to communicate by telepathy, sending messages across the distance of sea and land, and she did not mind talking about it. She kept notes of the communications she said she received and looked forward to comparing hers with those of her husband when she returned to New York. Mrs. Collins's nineteen-year-old daughter, named after her, was a quiet girl. She smiled at him shyly. Henry Coit, the Collinses' fifteen-year-old son, offered Luce his hand, as did Samuel Woodruff, the boy's uncle. He was traveling with the Collins party in the company of his wife.

Next, Luce shook hands with William Benedict Brown, at the age of twenty-nine the eldest son of James Brown. He was a strikingly handsome, practical man. Unlike Mrs. Collins, he did not believe in the supernatural. Several years earlier, while at Barnum's Museum in New York, he had had his palm read by a fortune-teller as a joke, without knowing, of course, that the incident would hold an eerie significance and that it forever after would haunt his friend, Howard Potter, who had accompanied him to the museum. The wrinkled old woman had stared up at him. When she had regained her composure, she solemnly said, "I see an awful shipwreck in your hand, sir." Amused, Brown had asked her for more specifics. The fortune-teller offered nothing more.

Brown was a man of the modern age, a true believer in the power of science and technology. Fortunes were to be made through hard work and intelligence. They were not predetermined, nor could they be discerned from the network of lines criss-crossing one's palm. He and his young wife, Clara, looked forward to a bright future. The previous year, Brown at last had been made a partner in his father's investment banking firm, Brown Brothers and Company, after proving himself capable of the duty required of him. He and Clara had a two-year-old daughter, Grace Alice Jane, who was in their stateroom in the company of her nurse. Luce greeted Clara warmly. She was French, with a fine nose and a buxom figure.

George Allen, William's brother-in-law, rose to offer Luce his hand. Allen was a tall man in his middle age, with a slightly weedy build and sharp features that gave him an almost birdlike countenance. He was an attorney and an associate of the Novelty Iron Works, the husband of Grace Brown, and the father of little Herbert, an infant approaching his first birthday. The baby was back in the Allens' stateroom with his nurse.

Grace and George, who had lost their previous two children while they were still infants, went to great efforts to keep Herbert warm, safe, and healthy. One of the reasons the Allen family was aboard *Arctic* stemmed from George's hope that an excursion might do Grace some good. By all appearances, it had. Herbert seemed to like traveling as well.

"And how is our guest of honor?" Luce asked Millie Brown, taking her hand in his.

Millie smiled. "The table looks splendid, Captain Luce. We are all so happy to be here on our way home."

Millie, her brother William, and her sister Grace, together with spouses and children, had been to England to visit their uncle, William Brown. Now seventy years old, Uncle William was one of four brothers who had come to the United States in 1802 to assist their father in his linen export business. The Browns originally hailed from Ireland, but unlike the millions who had come later in the century and found few opportunities upon their arrival in America, the Browns had carved out a handsome niche for themselves in high society.

The patriarch of the family, Alexander, started his commercial business in Belfast, then moved it across the ocean to Baltimore, Maryland, in 1800. A wise businessman, he soon discovered that the bales of cotton from the South amounted to nothing short of white gold if he could export them to England, where the Industrial Revolution and its resulting factories might turn the cotton into clothing for the middle classes on both sides of the Atlantic. Like so many other successful business ventures, timing was everything, and Alexander had been fortunate enough to get in on an industry about to explode in terms of its importance to the economies of Great Britain and the United States. With his four sons, of whom James Brown was the youngest, the Browns began exporting cotton to Liverpool and went on to found the largest and oldest privately owned investment banking company in North America. For a time, it was second only to the Bank of the United States, in which the family held a sizable share of stock as well.

As the Brown fortunes grew, Uncle William, the eldest son, returned to the Old World and put down roots in Liverpool. He presided over the Liverpool end of the family's burgeoning empire while his brothers took care of business in the company's branch offices in Baltimore, Philadelphia, New York, and Boston. Cotton built the Brown family, but banking propelled it into a status that even the old money of the big cities, those whose families settled on North American soil back in the 1600s, simply had to respect. Irish the Browns may have been, but they were not subjected to the derision and disrespect doled out to the newcomers fleeing the famine and unrest of Ireland in the late 1840s and early 1850s.

After Luce's greetings, the party began. The families and friends gave Millie a special birthday toast. They also toasted the good captain and his ship and raised glasses to the hope of another record-setting passage. The festivities continued for more than two hours, typical of the multicourse dinners served aboard *Arctic*. The pale light of late afternoon faded, illuminating the windows in shades of blue and gray. The lamps were lit, suffusing the natural light in bright yellow. Laughter rang out as the diners wound up their feast with port and cognac.

Not everyone aboard was in such a celebratory mood, nor was every passenger afforded the luxury of the fine dining in the saloon. The men, women, and children traveling aboard *Arctic* in second class satisfied themselves with the simpler, less expensive menu, with such basic fare as boiled beef, potatoes, and vegetables. There were no steerage passengers aboard the Collins ships. That trade was left to the packets and British steamship companies. Those in second class kept to themselves for the most part up in the forward part of the ship, in a sort of purgatory between the opulence of first class and the rough territory of the crew on the forecastle deck. One of these passengers was a young German sailor, Ferdinand Keyn.

Keyn traveled with a companion, his future boss, Captain Christianson, whose ship lay to her berth in Baltimore awaiting his return. At age twenty, Keyn already had five years of experience as a seaman sailing aboard ships from a variety of countries, and his ambition led him to seek a position aft in officers' country on the poop deck. At last, he had found an opportunity that promised him a steady climb in rank to end, finally, with a post as a master someday. After much hard work, he had saved the $80 for his fare on *Arctic* and a small stake to tide him over until he collected his first wages at his new job.

Keyn was better off than were some of the other passengers in the second-class cabin, having a place of employment even before setting foot in America. There were German, French, Italian, and Irish immigrants in second class, though not of the lower order, as the people in first class referred to the destitute found in cities from Hamburg to Bremen, Le Havre to Liverpool. Of them all, the German immigrants faced the best prospects. Because they brought skills to the United States and were excellent craftsmen, they were more well regarded and more easily assimilated into American culture than many others pursuing new lives in the New World. With the right kind of luck, Keyn might well improve his lot in life, and he was intelligent enough to realize that a man generally made his own destiny, be it good or bad, rich or poor.

Keyn had spent four times as much as the fare for steerage passengers on the packets, but the voyage across on the steamer was three times shorter. The accommodations were far more comfortable, and the food was better too. If he was to make a fresh start, Keyn determined to do so with as much dignity as possible. To cross an ocean crammed in the stinking hold of a sailing vessel for close to a month was unacceptable, particularly to a sailor who knew how bad it was for the people traveling down below. As he stood on deck, his pea coat protecting him from the cold made all the more intense by the ship's rapid progress through the sea, he watched the faint pricks of light on the shore grow smaller astern.

The twilight gave way to darkness as the hours passed, and *Arctic* fetched the eastern shore of Ireland. Luce appeared on deck often to monitor the ship's position through a process known as dead reckoning—simply knowing what direction you are going, at what speed, and for how long. He determined the vessel's speed every two hours with a device called a chip log. Together with the officer on watch, Luce ordered the log heaved astern and counted off the knots on the log line to gauge the velocity made good through the water. With this information, he calculated the distance made good in two hours and noted the estimated position on the chart, taking into account the set of the tide and the leeway that resulted from the force of the wind on the sails.

Under the lee of the Irish coast, the seas smoothed out and the ship approached her maximum speed of just over thirteen knots. While her passengers slept peacefully, the liner raced on through the night, and by dawn she drew near to Cape Clear. As the sun rose off her stern over the blue horizon, *Arctic*'s bow lifted to the first of the deep ocean swells rolling in from the North Atlantic without any land to obstruct and reduce their power. The motion was as familiar to Luce as his own bed in the large master suite at his home in Yonkers, as well known to him as the voice of his wife.

Arctic sped across the submerged lip of the continental shelf, making good time, reeling off daily runs of more than three hundred miles. Day by day, the Grand Banks of Newfoundland drew closer. In less than a month, when all of New York, all of the United States, and much of the world learned of her tragic fate, an anonymous poet would write in the *Herald:*

> . . . No one dreamed
> That, brooding darkly o'er the vessel's bow,
>   Fate hung in gloom, while death, with close veiled head,
> Crouched like a phantom on the pointed prow.

CHAPTER EIGHT

COLLISION COURSE

A S WAS HIS HABIT, Captain Luce awoke before dawn on September 27. He viewed his early morning ritual as part of his duty to the safety of his ship and passengers. But there was another reason for waking early, one more psychological in nature than the usual activities associated with his rank, the day-to-day management of the ship, keeping records, tending to navigation. It did the men under his command good to observe him about the decks at all hours, lest they think him predictable and find ways to slack off when they thought he might not notice. Although he had retired early, the restless night tossing and turning in his bunk left him feeling groggy and somehow ill at ease. A portrait of a vigilant captain, he rubbed the sleep from his eyes, yawned, and stretched the stiffness from his arms and legs.

Despite the heat from the radiator in his cabin and the protection of his long underwear, Luce felt chilled as he threw off the heavy wool blankets and quickly pulled on his pantaloons, laced his shoes, and slipped into his starched white shirt. He tied a black cravat loosely around his neck and put on his vest, jacket, and pea coat. He looked in the mirror, combed his hair, and set his cap on his head at a slight angle, giving him the rakish nautical look he liked.

At seven days out, he and the rest of the ship's company found their clothing heavy with the odor of their own bodies. They had not bathed in freshwater since leaving port. In summer, sometimes the male passengers took advantage of a seawater bath while the crew holystoned the deck before breakfast. Few wanted to avail themselves of one in autumn. He looked forward to a long, hot soak in the tub as soon as he arrived home. Although *Arctic* was built for comfort and convenience, she could not match the shoreside amenities available in the better homes of the city, some of which boasted such luxuries as central heating and running water.

Luce emerged from his cabin to find the deck lanterns glowing like little suns amid the swirl of a dense fog that created halos around each of them. The gray mist did not linger around the lights, though, as it might on a still evening on the streets of New York, Liverpool, and Le Havre. Instead, the fog rode a moderate westerly wind coming in at an angle off the bow. The ship's forward momentum through the water added to its strength, almost doubling its velocity, and inspired the impression that the air thick with moisture flowed like a river across the decks to disappear into the black void that surrounded her on all sides.

Luce walked to the rail and gazed off into the gloom, shivering slightly from the dampness. He could not see the long ocean swells through the darkness and fog, but he felt them roll in under *Arctic's* quarter from a southeasterly direction in opposition to the westerly wind. He knew the signs that heralded the presence of a distant storm system gathering strength astern many miles away—the dog before the master, as the sailors called it. Always before a big wind came, the swells foretold its arrival. He wondered if the steamer might outrun the approaching gale or at least make westing enough to duck its full fury. One never could count on such a thing aboard a sailing ship, but aboard a swift steamer, the possibility of dodging heavy weather did in fact exist. It was just another example of how the modern age had turned traditional seamanship upside down and added a new way to cope with the ocean's occasional ugly moods.

It had been a routine passage thus far, with the usual patches of rough weather that worried the passengers who were not accustomed to the North Atlantic. Even after all these years, the fear on the faces of the men and women as they experienced the full magnitude of an angry sea moved Luce to compassion and a desire to allay the concerns of those in his charge. He sat with them in the saloon and adopted a bold demeanor for their benefit. A steamship, he said, was far safer than the sailing packets. With powerful engines, a captain might stand a chance to avoid mishaps even if faced with a lee shore. Under sail alone, the wind could easily drive a ship onto a rocky coast to leeward, and it often did. Statistically, an average of one out of six American sailing packets went down during their long years of service, and these crack vessels were considered safer than the regular traders, which were not always well maintained and staffed with experienced mariners on the poop deck. The casualty rate for these vessels, particularly those engaged in the immigrant trade, was much higher.

Of the nine sailing ships of the Red Star Line and other companies Luce had served aboard as master prior to taking command of *Arctic*, seven of them had sunk after he left them in the care of another captain. His command previous to *Constellation, John R. Skiddy*, had gone down with considerable loss of life off the southeast coast of Ireland. Under sail, a captain faced a narrow range of options to avoid calamity. Foul winds and heavy seas could drive ships on the rocks with little or no recourse for her commander. Even the best seamen could not always claw off a lee shore, at least not without the help of engines to drive a ship against wind and sea.

Major disasters in the transatlantic steamship trade were not very common. True, some vessels ran hard aground like the *City of Philadelphia* had done off Cape Race several weeks past in August 1854. The steamer was deemed a total loss, but the incident did not result in any deaths. Luce himself was not infallible. In May 1854, he managed to drive *Arctic* up onto Tuscar Rock off the south coast of Ireland. He backed her off quickly enough, but being a prudent captain, he returned to Liverpool to have the steamer checked carefully for structural damage before setting off across the Atlantic. None was found, and he proceeded on to New York. This was the first accident in his more than three years as *Arctic*'s captain, and it humbled him. Other commanders were not as lucky. The British ship *City of Glasgow*, of the Inman Line, sailed from Liverpool in March 1854 with a company of 480 men, women, and children and disappeared without a trace. It was one of the rare instances that a mighty steamer went missing in the sixteen years since oceangoing steamships had been in regular service.

The sea was a dangerous place. There was no denying it. The great advances in shipbuilding and the improvements of marine steam engines diminished the danger, but the North Atlantic would always remain inhospitable and unforgiving. As if to confirm this fact, Luce's efforts to instill confidence in his passengers during rough weather were frequently ineffectual. The violent motion of the ship, the howling wind and driving spray, the incessant roar of the gale in the rigging, and the mountainous waves marching relentlessly toward the vessel drove home the point to the most hardened traveler that even a large steamer represented nothing of significance when put up against the vast forces of the ocean.

Abbott wrote an apt description of just what it was like aboard *Arctic* at the height of a storm, with vivid recollection of the discomfort and a dash of humor as well. He reported on the difficulties of trying to dine, the plates sliding to and fro on the table against the fiddles meant to stop the china from falling to the floor, and tea or coffee taking flight just as the cup was lifted. Even walking became an acrobatic exercise:

> You start to cross the saloon; a wave lifts the stern of the ship some twenty feet into the air, and you find yourself pitching down a steep hill. You lean back as far as possible to preserve your balance, when suddenly another wave, with gigantic violence, thrusts up the bows of the ship, and you have a precipitous eminence before you. Just as you are recovering from your astonishment, the ship takes a lurch, and, to your utter confusion, you find yourself floundering in a lady's lap, who happens to be reading upon a sofa on one side of the saloon. Hardly have you commenced your apology ere another wave

comes kindly to your rescue, and pitches you bodily out of the door.

The drama of such moments was offset with the seemingly slow passage of time when the sea calmed down and there was not fear of the elements for distraction:

Life upon the sea is indeed monotonous, as hour after hour, and day after day, lingers along, and you look out only upon the chill dreary expanse of wintery waves, and the silent or stormy sky. . . . Groups of ladies and gentlemen are gathered upon the sofas [in the saloon], some reading, some talking, some playing various games. . . . There is, however, an amazing fondness for champagne and tobacco. Were Byron here, he would, without doubt, correct his celebrated line, "Man, thou pendulum betwixt a smile and a tear," into, "Man, thou pendulum betwixt the wine glass and the cigar."

So it was for the passengers of *Arctic*. Luce observed the social gatherings in the saloons and participated in them when he felt it was his duty or he was inclined to do so of his own accord. He spent much time with Millie Brown talking with her on deck, together with his son. Luce showed her the parts of the ship usually off-limits to the passengers, which delighted her. The closer *Arctic* drew to the North American coast, the happier Millie became. He noted with a smile and an almost paternal protectiveness the budding romance between her and a handsome stockbroker, William Gilbert, a man known to the Brown family from his dealings on Wall Street. He moved in the banking world with a confidence that earned him respect among the upper class, though to a common man he counted as nothing more than a dandy or a swell whose smooth, clean hands smacked of femininity. Members of the Brown family later reported that they were often seen on deck together engrossed in animated conversation. There were even rumors that the two might be planning to announce their engagement, possibly accounting for Millie's high spirits.

Millie said she missed her parents, and her two younger brothers, George and John, who had returned home from England several weeks earlier to start the school year. They both had wished to remain with Millie, Grace, and William so they could all come home together aboard *Arctic*, but a stern headmaster and their parents' insistence that they not miss any time at school had overruled their desire to extend their time in Europe with their siblings as long as possible. Millie looked forward to a family reunion upon the ship's arrival at New York. She had been away from family and friends for most of the summer and had much to catch up on.

According to records passed down to relatives in the Brown family, Millie's parents expressed misgivings about her joining the rest of the party on a visit to Europe. The reason for their concern remains unknown, but they clearly did not want her to go, quite possibly because she was a favorite of James Brown, her father, and with the rest of his children and grandchildren away from home her presence might make their absence easier to bear. They relented only after George Allen and Grace promised to protect her and bring her safely back to New York.

Millie was said to have faced the prospect of travel with guarded enthusiasm. The night before the Brown and Allen families set sail aboard *Arctic* bound for Liverpool, Millie's mother and father threw a party. One of the guests was Charles C. Nott. He described that last evening in a letter, written in his old age to James Brown's daughter-in-law on May 27, 1912, and published in *The American Neptune* in 1959. Nott had known Millie when she was a young girl. She caught his fancy even before she grew up to become a vivacious, beautiful woman. He characterized her as the most "happy and healthy . . . human being" he had ever known, "unfailing in her cheerfulness" and a person who even as a girl could "listen and talk like a woman."

At the end of the party, Millie accompanied Nott to the door. They were alone together on the stairway leading to the entry hall, with Millie leaning on the banister, Nott just below her on the stairs looking up at her. They talked about nothing serious, just their shared displeasure at how some of their friends and relatives who had gone to England had come home with some of the English prejudices against the United States, how it was uncivilized and backward compared to Great Britain and its growing empire.

"And Millie Brown, whatever you do or don't do, don't come back with any prejudices against your Country," Nott said.

Millie answered him, her voice sad, so sad in fact that Nott vividly remembered it fifty-eight years later. "I shall never do that," she said. As wealthy as her family was, they were still Irish. They had come from a land where class prejudices denied freedom and opportunity to an entire people, and they had found in America, in spite of its faults, a place where individuals were free to make their mark on the world. While Millie moved in the moneyed circle of the elite, she remained sensitive to her roots and harbored an intense patriotic fervor for the United States and all it had given her family.

Nott was struck by the tone of Millie's voice as she spoke. He thought there was meaning in it, an unspoken message. In his letter, Nott wrote: "I . . . thought she was a little homesick before she started [on the trip] and secretly wishing that she were not going. I think so still." If Nott's recollections were correct, it was not surprising Millie's spirits grew brighter as the ship neared land, the journey almost done, her future bright with the promise of a burgeoning romance with the handsome young stockbroker, William Gilbert.

By this time, Luce had gotten to know some of the other important passengers sailing aboard *Arctic*. Among them was a young diplomat from France headed to Washington, D.C., on official business, Robert Christian Godefroy Fernanad de Gramont, duc de Caderousse. Only twenty, he possessed a debonair flash and pomp that pleased the ladies. He traveled with his manservant, who was in constant attendance.

Other interesting characters included railroad promoters, publishers, physicians, lawyers, artists, merchants, and several professors from American universities. One of them was Henry Hope Reed, a professor of rhetoric and English literature on the staff of the University of Pennsylvania. He was quite fond of talking about his favorite English poet and close personal friend, the late William Wordsworth, an American edition of whose works Reed had recently edited. He prattled on about Wordsworth and his philosophy to a painful and somewhat self-important degree. Some of the passengers avoided him and pitied the young lady who traveled with him, a Miss Bronson, the sister of Reed's wife.

Luce knew of two ladies among his passengers due to their high social standing in New York City. Mrs. Scott, the widow of a major killed in the Mexican War, traveled with her brother, an amiable gentleman from the Midwest. Mrs. Ropes traveled with her eight-year-old son, who, like Willie, was in poor health. His mother thought a trip to Europe and a sea passage might improve his spirits, and evidently the boy was as enthralled with the adventure as Willie was. Mr. Ropes was awaiting the return of his wife and only child back in New York.

Of particular interest to Luce was a Captain D. Pratt. Several weeks earlier, Pratt's ship had foundered at sea during a storm, and it was only by chance that he and his wife and child were rescued. The two commanders talked much of the dangers of the North Atlantic and the strange way it spared some while taking others. The randomness of life and death at sea disturbed their Victorian sense of order and defied the perception that a benevolent God watched over his flock with an equal love for all. Of the more than 400 souls aboard were a large number of entire family units—husbands and wives, many with their children, sisters and brothers, uncles and aunts, nephews and nieces—traveling together. The families made friends as the voyage progressed. In all, it was a convivial and civil scene on the decks and in the saloons.

Shaking off his thoughts of the voyage and home, Luce turned away from the rail and strode briskly to the chart house. On the chart table was a gray rectangle of slate. Written on it in chalk were the remarks from the officers, a running tally of the ship's progress that was summarized and entered into the official log once each day. Luce scanned the notes on the course, wind and sea conditions, the ship's speed, and estimated position. The day before, the weather cleared enough for him to take a sufficient number of observations with his sextant to fix his position at approximately three hundred miles east northeast of Cape Race, the southeastern extremity of Newfoundland. *Arctic*'s heading would take her straight across the shallow, plankton-rich waters of the Grand Banks, which had lured fishermen to the area since the 1500s. There the continental shelf of North America reached far out to sea and created an ideal habitat to support the food chain.

The Grand Banks represented a crossroads for transatlantic shipping as well as a robust fishery for Canada, Great Britain, the United States, France, Spain, and Portugal. Vessels bound for Quebec or Montreal on the St. Lawrence River proceeded on through Cabot Strait into the Gulf of St. Lawrence. Those bound for Halifax, Nova Scotia, laid a more west-southwesterly course, and those headed for Boston and New York followed almost the same track before diverging in the Gulf of Maine to make for their respective ports of call. All the tracks came together off Cape Race, and because of the heavy traffic, the waters that *Arctic* now traversed were among the most dangerous on earth. They demanded the respect of mariners, as did the ocean off Cape Horn at the southern tip of South America.

The pervasive fog on the Grand Banks made navigation all the more difficult. The frigid waters of the Labrador Current swept southward from the Arctic along the coasts of Labrador and Newfoundland to meet the tropical waters brought thousands of miles from the Sargasso Sea from the strong flow of the Gulf Stream. These two ocean currents converged on the Grand Banks, creating violent localized weather systems and, more frequently, blankets of thick fog that lasted for weeks at a stretch. Even a stiff southerly wind, which might disperse fog on the coast of New England, served only to make the weather all the more dense on the banks. Instead of looming over the sea in quiet repose, the fog blew sideways at twenty to thirty knots in what sailors called a smoky sou'wester.

Adding to the danger of heavy shipping traffic and fog, icebergs often rode the Labrador Current far to the south, particularly in spring. They had been sighted as far below the Grand Banks as a latitude of forty degrees north, and they posed a significant hazard to vessels traveling the great circle route between European and North American ports. On April 14, 1912, the British liner *Titanic* struck an iceberg approximately four hundred miles southeast of Newfoundland, well within the boundaries of the ice limit but well away from the shallows of the Grand Banks toward which *Arctic* steamed at full speed. She sank with a loss of 1,517 lives, evidence that ocean travel on the northern shipping lanes remained dangerous fifty-eight years later.

Luce had always been uneasy about speeding through these waters in thick weather. He knew the fishermen dreaded the approach of a transatlantic steamer. Many a schooner went missing, crushed without even raising alarm aboard the much larger liners. The steamers smashed them to pulp or cut them in half and proceeded on their way with no one aware of the death that lay in the wake. Luce knew that the pilots from Halifax, Boston, and sometimes even New York, all of whom could be found on the banks, shared a similar dread of these freight trains of the sea. A wise pilot positioned his schooner to ensure her bow and stern faced the well-traveled shipping lanes rather than lying beam to and increasing the odds of a collision.

While knowing full well the dangers, Luce and his colleagues tried not to think about them very much. They were under orders to make fast passages regardless of heavy weather, fog, or ice. The transatlantic shipping companies mutely accepted the risks of harming a small craft, perhaps killing her crew or stranding them on the oily swells of the North Atlantic in their little dories. It was all part of doing business in the modern age. Of all the companies, the Collins Line ranked as the most fanatical about maintaining its schedules and setting records whenever possible.

As *Arctic* sped along that early morning, the sky to the east astern grown pale white and gray on the horizon as the sun began to rise, Luce sent word to the two lookouts on the bow to keep a weather eye out for other ships. It was all he could do from a practical standpoint. *Arctic* was not equipped with a steam whistle. In fact, most oceangoing steamers did not use them, though they were common on river steamboats operating in restricted waterways.

Aside from the ship's bell, most often mounted on the forecastle deck, the only means of making an auditory warning were signal cannons and tin horns powered with the breath of the lookout. When working in confined waters in thick weather, captains sometimes ordered lookouts to use the horns, but few did so on the high seas. No laws existed to decide the matter for the steamship master, and most of them considered the horns useless when cruising at full speed. The sound could not possibly carry far enough to herald an imminent collision in time for anyone to avoid it.

In addition, the concept of traffic separation zones, where westbound vessels kept to a specific lane and eastbound vessels kept to another, was completely alien to mariners of the mid-1850s. Established shipping lanes with separation zones were soon proposed, however, and adopted in the years shortly after 1854. Samuel Cunard would take action before the concept of separation zones was widely accepted, building his reputation as a safety-conscious owner. He would order his captains to steer courses along predetermined lanes, and he advertised this practice to make other mariners aware of when, where, and from which direction they might encounter a Cunard liner between New York and Liverpool. In the mid-1850s, Cunard's safety record was unmatched. Since his company had gone into operation more than a decade before, he had never lost a ship, the life of a passenger due to nautical mishap, or a single shipment of mail. Yet even his ships were not operating as safely as possible. Oceangoing liners were not legally required to carry enough lifeboats to ensure that everyone aboard would have a seat in the event of an emergency. Not much changed in this regard until *Titanic* sank in 1912, repeating the same mistake that led to the tragedy that would soon occur aboard *Arctic* as she steamed toward Cape Race on that foggy September morning in 1854. The shortcomings of maritime safety were about to become clear. The danger of ships crisscrossing each other's courses as a matter of routine was no longer to be simply ignored.

The passengers stirred awake as the sky grew lighter and the fog swept in and out like a curtain rising and falling on an empty stage. They talked quietly among themselves, waiting for the gong to sound for breakfast at eight o'clock. The ship had sped through fog on several occasions during her crossing. On this morning, however, one passenger, a Scotsman by the name of James Smith traveling in second class who had crossed the Atlantic on nine occasions, was concerned. He felt "somewhat astonished and alarmed several times when on deck, seeing the weather so thick, that I fancied not more than three or four of the ship's lengths ahead could be seen, and she going at full speed, without any alarm bell, steam whistle or other signal being sounded at intervals, in some such manner as I had been accustomed to in a fog on other vessels."

The breakfast hour came and went, the crew assigned to the forenoon watch mustered for duty, and the passengers settled in to their amusements on a dreary morning. The sun rose higher and illuminated the sky above the steamer in a dome of bright blue that became white and gray and impenetrable toward the surface of the sea, its building waves visible for just a few dozen yards on either side of the vessel. The steady wash of the bow wave and the splash of the paddle wheels seemed muffled in the heavy, thick air. The fog closed in until the bow of the steamer disappeared, and just as quickly it lifted again to reveal the confused seas, short and steep from the influence of the shoal water, the opposing wind and swell, and the force of the tide that ran swiftly on the banks. At times, the breaks in the fog extended the visible horizon out to almost two miles.

Just before noon, a group of passengers met in the dining saloon to wait for the arrival of Captain Luce. It was a daily ritual. Every day at around lunchtime the captain announced how many miles the ship had made good during the previous twenty-four hours and gave them their approximate distance from port. Those passengers who were interested put money in a pool and drew numbers from a hat. The person with the number closest to the day's tally won the lottery, sometimes a substantial sum. The people who waited for Luce talked and drank together, paying no attention to the world outside the warm, brightly lit saloon.

Out on deck, Captain Luce smiled as he lifted his sextant and shot the sun as it reached its highest point in the sky for September 27 in their current location. This was known as local noon. He was pleased to have obtained the observation. It would help him fix the ship's position relative to the rapidly approaching rocky coast. The fog closed in thick again, but he relaxed a little, knowing he would soon have a precise determination of where he was. He walked briskly to the chart house and sat down to work out the complicated figures required to break down a celestial observation without the aid of modern sight reduction tables, a lengthy calculation involving plane geometry and spherical trigonometry. He was still there a quarter of an hour later.

At twelve-fifteen, up forward in his stateroom near the bow, James Smith sat bolt upright. He clearly heard the lookout call out in a panic, "Stop her! Stop her! A steamer ahead!" The cry was "heard with alarm by myself and all others in the cabin, at the same time the man giving the alarm could be heard running off towards the engine room. I stepped out of my stateroom, and with Mr. Cook, my room-mate, [tried] to calm the excitement among the ladies in the cabin."

Standing on the paddle-wheel box, the officer of the deck, upon hearing the lookout's warning, strained to see ahead in the fog. Out of the mist loomed the form of a little propeller-driven steamship rigged with three masts. She sailed under full canvas, the wind off her quarter. Black smoke carried forward over her bow and merged with the fog, indicating she also steamed along under full power. She came at *Arctic* making better than ten knots at an oblique angle just off the starboard bow, though very nearly on a direct collision course bow to bow.

The officer had a split second to decide whether to turn to starboard or to port. Either way, it would be close, very close. He may well have had the impulse to steer across the steamship's bow to allow her to pass close aboard along *Arctic's* port side. The angle was shorter, requiring the liner to make less of a turn to take her out of danger. But to do so would break a cardinal rule of the sea: Never turn toward an oncoming vessel. In compliance with his training, he shouted, "Hard starboard!" to the mate on deck. The mate yanked the bell pull. One bell clanged in the wheel house. The helmsman spun the wheel to the right.

The officer's order might confuse modern readers. In the nineteenth century, a ship's wheel did not operate like a car in that turning it left would steer it to the left. It was set up so that to turn the vessel left, or to port, one had to turn the wheel to the right. Thus, for the officer to order *Arctic* turned to port he had to tell the helmsman to turn the wheel to starboard. The system dated back to a time when vessels were much smaller and required no mechanical advantage to move the rudder. In those days, a long piece of wood known as a tiller was attached to the top of the rudder. Pushing the tiller to the right turned the ship to the left, and pushing the tiller to the left turned the ship to the right. Not until 1924, with the proliferation of the automobile, were the helms on ships set up to steer like cars.

Hearing the officer's command, Luce jumped from his chair in the chart house, aware that something was going terribly wrong.

The two ships closed. Fifty yards. Twenty. Ten.

Francis Dorian, the third mate, heard the warning cry from his position below decks. He was new to *Arctic*, having been transferred from *Atlantic* eight months earlier. A native of Ireland, he had brought his family over to America several years past and together with his wife and children built a life of modest comfort. At age thirty-four, Dorian's career lagged behind that of many other mariners. Yet he had worked

Disaster on the Grand Banks

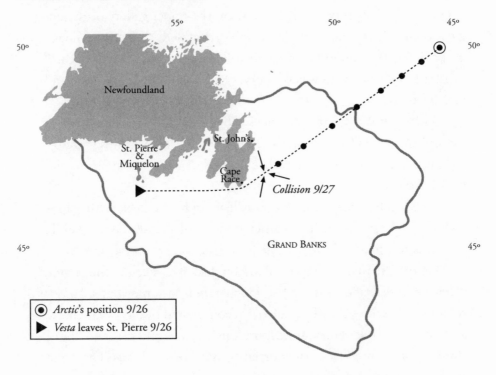

Newfoundland

St. John's

St. Pierre
&
Miquelon

Cape
Race

Collision 9/27

GRAND BANKS

- ⊙ *Arctic's* position 9/26
- ▶ *Vesta* leaves St. Pierre 9/26

hard and achieved a posting on one of the most famous ships in the world. He was content with his lot in life. Upon hearing the panicked call of the officer on watch, Dorian rushed topside and arrived on deck before Captain Luce did.

"The first I heard was the cry, 'Hard starboard,' and then understood that there was something wrong. I went on deck and found the vessels about seven yards apart. I stood watching the Arctic, in the full expectation that she should yield her helm [turn just in time to avoid the collision]."

The distance closed fast. Not more than a minute had elapsed since the initial warning. The officer on deck knew the two ships were about to collide, that his gamble had not paid off. *Arctic* did not turn fast enough. "Stop her! Stop her!" he screamed. The mate signaled the engine room. Down below at his post on the upper gallery of the engine room, Chief Engineer J. W. Rogers grumbled, "What's up now?" as the bell rang to order full stop. He called out to James Willett, third assistant engineer, who was on duty. "Unhook her, Mr. Willett, and look lively there!"

"Full astern!" the officer on deck called. But it was too late. Even as the signal reached the men in the engine room, the two ships met bow to bow before *Arctic*'s paddle wheels could slow her momentum and back her clear.

Luce reached the companionway leading to the deck as the ships collided and saw the little steamer forward of the starboard paddle wheel, as she grazed along the side of the ship on her way astern.

"Before the man giving the alarm on deck had reached the engine room we were made aware of the concussion by a somewhat slight jar to our ship," James Smith recalled, "accompanied by a crashing noise against the starboard bow. It was a moment of awe and suspense, but I think we all seemed to satisfy ourselves that the shock was slight, and that as we were on so large and strong a vessel, no serious damage had happened, or could well happen to such a ship."

James Smith was not the only person aboard *Arctic* to believe she had come through the collision without suffering severe damage. The ship's officers, passengers, and crew thought themselves safe. But a short time after the collision with the French steamship *Vesta*, their immediate jeopardy became starkly obvious.

CHAPTER NINE

THE FISHERMAN'S ESCAPE

WITH THE ARRIVAL OF FALL on the Grand Banks, the nights grew longer, plunging the region into its early stages of winter darkness when the wan sun, always weak, provided even less comfort than it did during the cold summers. The fog and gales swept in turn over the high bluffs of the Newfoundland coast and created an enhanced sense of isolation for the band of French fishermen living on the tiny islands of St. Pierre and Miquelon lying about ten miles west of the Burin peninsula separating Fortune and Placentia bays. The timeless cycle of the changing seasons and the onset of inhospitable weather on the banks gave impetus to another annual occurrence: the exodus of many of the fishermen from the islands. It signified an end to the months of toil in their dories and schooners and an end of work for the salters ashore tending the racks used to dry the cod recently hauled from the depths.

The huts clustered on the shores of St. Pierre emptied as the men cleared out, bound for home on the ships their employers sent to collect them at season's end. The largest town on St. Pierre, with its well-protected harbor, continued to bustle. It served as a major point of embarkation for the fishermen. Crowds of them gathered there to board the ships. Among them was a veteran of the Grand Banks trade, a short, stocky man in his later years, Jassonet François. He carried to the quay his duffel of ragged clothing rank with the odor of fish, along with his equally odoriferous bedding. He nursed a fervent hope that the market in Europe for the salt cod and barrels of cod liver oil might reward him with a tidy sum to support his family through another long winter before he returned to St. Pierre the following spring. He was a native of a little village near Saint-Malo in northwest France, and the seasonal work on the Grand Banks was the only life he knew.

Gone were the days when the French ruled these northern reaches of the North American continent, although they had been among the first to see the value of the Grand Banks fishery, followed by the Portuguese, Spanish, and British. As early as 1517, large numbers of Frenchmen ventured across the western ocean to fish for cod. The harbor of refuge at Le Havre was constructed in part to support the companies dispatching vessels to harvest the rich catches on the banks, and in 1635 the French established a permanent settlement on St. Pierre. The rivalry and frequent hostilities between France and Great Britain, however, chipped away at the French holdings, until finally the two islands remained their sole outpost in the northern parts of the New World. Small as the foothold may have been, it was still an important economic resource for French entrepreneurs.

One such company was Hernoux & Cie of Dieppe. One of the wealthiest firms in France engaged in the Grand Banks fishery, the proprietors thought nothing of spending a portion of their profits to build and equip the best ships for the service. In 1853, they commissioned a yard in Nantes, France, to build them a new ship to serve as a tender for their employees on St. Pierre. They spent much capital on her construction and adopted the state of the art in terms of shipbuilding technology, doing away with the old-fashioned paddle wheels in favor of a propeller driven by a 60-horsepower auxiliary steam engine. The vessel carried a large spread of canvas set on three masts.

At 250 gross tons, the ship's iron hull stretched to 152 feet on deck and was fitted inside with three watertight bulkheads, another significant step forward in the new way of things in the modern age: the use of iron and watertight compartments. As wood suitable for shipbuilding grew scarcer in Great Britain and France in the 1850s, iron became the preferred material for the stout vessels needed to cross oceans. Great Britain, with its burgeoning iron foundries, stood at the forefront of this new technology. In 1821, its builders launched the world's first vessel built completely of iron. They were also quick to adopt the propeller, which was to prove far more efficient than the paddle wheel.

Although there were many initial skeptics of iron for use in ship construction, they were disappearing fast as the advantages of iron became obvious. An iron ship was stronger and easier to repair than one made of wood, and it was also lighter because less iron was required to maintain the integrity of the hull. Across the Atlantic, however, where the forests remained seemingly limitless, the preferred building material was still wood, and the idea that watertight compartments might prove useful was frequently dismissed as an unnecessary complication of an age-old form. Although she was built for possible use during a war, *Arctic* was not designed with watertight bulkheads. Her hold was open from stem to stern.

When the vessel was completed, the company christened her *Vesta* and brought aboard an experienced master to command her, Captain Alphonse Duchesne. He was a tall, big-boned man with a bold oval face, a receding hairline, a trim mustache, and a goatee. He looked the part of a French gentleman and was capable of dealing with the wealthy owners of Hernoux & Cie in a manner that pleased their sense of civility. But he was also just as capable of knocking down an unruly member of his fifty-man crew with a belaying pin or taking care of the offender with his bare hands.

Vesta put to sea on September 26 and made good progress along the southern coast of Newfoundland. By the morning of September 27, she sailed fast before a moderate wind bound on the great circle route to France. Among her 147 fishermen and salters was Jassonet François. He sat on deck with most of the other passengers to escape the damp confines of the ship's interior. In this foggy and cold weather, the iron sides of the vessel streamed with condensation. Everything inside was wet and smelled of fish, sweat, and sodden wool. The men were used to the unpleasant weather on the banks; they preferred it to the cramped quarters below. All appeared well. The men smoked, talked quietly, and thought longingly of the women waiting for them in France.

Up forward on the forecastle deck, two lookouts stood watch. By order of their captain, they lifted their spyglasses every minute or so to peer into the fog banks swirling before them. The acrid sting of coal smoke from the stack made their eyes water as it wafted past on the following breeze. The wash of the bow wave mingled with the thrum of the rigging and the occasional flutter of canvas as the crew adjusted the trim of the sails. *Vesta* rose and fell, rolling to the swells washing in toward her from the open sea. Spray pattered on the foredeck and water dripped from the fore stays and the bellies of the headsails eased fair to catch the wind.

Suddenly, a dark shape materialized through the fog. Both lookouts lifted their glasses. But it disappeared. The fog played tricks with the eye, bending shapes and casting shadows. It muffled the sound of the waves and the voices of men on deck, and deflected the sound to make it seem as if it came from a distant source. The lookouts waited, slightly tense now, for the next break in the dense wall of gray in front of their ship. They listened intently for some sound that should not be there—the rush of another vessel's bow wave, the rhythmic slap of paddle wheels, or perhaps the bleat of a tin horn.

Then the curtain of fog tore open, and a moment later the towering black form of a steamship loomed above both lookouts. Frozen in fear, they simply watched it, the froth of white foam churning at the bow, the two huge wheels visible on either side of the oncoming vessel headed almost directly for them bow on. Stirred to action in seconds, the lookouts cried out, "Luff! Luff! There is a ship bearing down upon us!"

Jassonet François craned his neck to look up at the bow of the other ship, which appeared to soar skyward like a black cliff with surf breaking at its base. He jumped to his feet with the other men. He saw the lookouts hesitate, then run aft. The other ship began to turn. She rode up on the back of a large swell, exposing the dark green of her copper sheathing, just as *Vesta* slid down into the trough. The French steamer rose as the other ship fell. Their bows met a second later with stupendous force.

The impact stopped *Vesta* dead in the water and caused a high-pitched, piercing shriek as the iron plates ripped apart and the frames and stem bent and twisted. The noise was terrifying and loud enough to hurt Jassonet François's ears. The bow folded inward on itself for at least ten feet, taking the foremast down. The rigging whipped through the air with a sickening whir and slashed at the sails set on the mainmast, tearing them to shreds. The ship lifted up as if on a wave. More of the bow crumpled and compressed back, maiming some of the less agile crewmen who had been knocked down from the shock and could not get out of the way fast enough. The jagged sharp edges of the torn metal impaled one of them. His screams filled the air, but did not last long. Blood pooled on the weather deck aft of what was left of the forecastle. Some of the wounded writhed in the scuppers, with arms and legs broken, the bones protruding from their soiled clothing and flesh.

The rest of the passengers and crew wailed in panic and milled around. They pleaded to God to save them. They cried for their mothers, wives, lovers, and sisters, thinking they had but moments to live. *Vesta* hit the steamer's side again and again, before she bounced off the guards protecting the liner's starboard paddle wheel and sheared off astern as the other vessel plowed forward into the fog. She vanished for a moment and just as quickly reappeared, moving more slowly and starting to turn toward them.

Captain Duchesne's voice roared from the poop deck, demanding that everyone stay calm until the mates ascertained the true extent of the damage below the waterline and whether the forward watertight compartment was still intact and holding. If it held, he might just save the ship. A crewman rushed from the hatchway leading to the hold and yelled, "She's filling up with water! She's filling!" The panic increased exponentially.

Fishermen, salters, and crew bolted for the lifeboats. Armed with belaying pins, Duchesne and the mates tried to block them. They succeeded in stopping all hands from reaching all but two of the boats. Crazed with fear, the men who had eluded the mates did not even finish clearing the first boat away before several leaped from Vesta's side into it. The boat teetered below the davits, swinging back and forth by the falls, and capsized. Men hit the water and thrashed about, drowning each other as they grabbed for anything to keep them afloat. In minutes, they all died. Bodies floated astern.

Jassonet François forced his way through the mass of teeming men, beating and kicking a path to the rail. He jumped into the second boat just as it cleared the deck, along with seven others. Duchesne bellowed at them to stop as they lowered away. The boat splashed into the waves. They cut the falls, unshipped the oars, and began to row as fast as they could toward the big steamship they thought must save them after Vesta soon sank with all hands. Duchesne ordered them to stand by the ship to help save their friends and countrymen. They heard his curses, damning them to hell. Each stroke of the oars brought them closer to the American vessel, already an indistinct black shadow in the whirls and eddies of the fog.

Facing aft in the boat, each at his seat laying to the oars with a will, they saw Duchesne at the taffrail raise his fist and strike the air. But they did not care to listen to him. His form soon merged with the others on deck and grew faint in the churning vapor shooting across the swells. They had little time to reach the steamer before they lost their way and faced the dangerous prospect of drifting alone on the open sea in a boat without provisions or even a compass to guide them. As for the probable fate of their countrymen, it was just the way of it at sea. Some men lived; others died. It had always been so and would always be so. The men strained at the oars and put any thought of turning back, if such a pang of conscience ever surfaced, as far from their minds as possible. If their actions were dishonorable, far more dishonor was to befall seamen that day.

CHAPTER TEN

A NOBLE GESTURE

CAPTAIN LUCE paused for a moment at the rail, scarcely believing the sight of the stricken steamer drifting off astern, her bow a mass of torn and crumpled iron, a gaping hole through which torrents of water flowed as if over the lip of a dam or the edge of a waterfall. He could actually see crates, boxes, and casks floating in the ship's hold. Already *Vesta* seemed well down at the bow. Her decks swarmed with men. He could hear their calls. Although he did not understand French, he knew they begged for help, that their ship must soon sink beneath the waves. A hole as large as that meant the men aboard the vessel had only a few more minutes to live. Luce was not alone in his conclusion.

The male passengers were among the first to come out on deck to see what had happened, leaving the ladies talking excitedly in the saloons. Stockbroker William Gilbert was seated in the dining saloon with Clara Brown, Grace Brown Allen, Millie Brown, and other friends just before the collision. Gilbert described what he saw when he reached the deck with the other men:

> Immediately after the collision, all the gentlemen ran on deck, and we saw indistinctly through the mist, on our starboard quarter, a propeller with her bow, to all appearance, completely knocked out. So badly did she appear to be injured, that it was the impression of all on the Arctic that she must sink. The hole in her was large enough to admit the water in immense volumes, and through it, her lading could be seen

down to the water's edge. . . . For the first fifteen minutes after the collision, not realizing that we were in any danger, I did not pay much attention to what was passing, being most of the time with the ladies, who in the mean time had come up from the saloon.

In those first few minutes, an increasing number of those on *Arctic* stood along her rails and shared Luce's horror at the sight of the French steamship. Many looked on the scene with a sense of wonder, much the same way modern travelers on a highway staring at the mangled wrecks of cars, the occupants laid out on the pavement with emergency technicians in attendance, experience a mixture of horror and the odd though natural tendency to feel grateful to have escaped such mayhem themselves. The plight of the vessel represented a strange sort of unexpected entertainment, a break, however unwelcome because of its tragic nature, from the boredom of shipboard life.

Luce ran up the stairs to the top of the starboard paddle-wheel box, joining the officer on deck, who stared at *Vesta* in utter disbelief at the extent of the damage. Luce peered over the side. The guards fore and aft of the paddle wheel were splintered, and he could make out what he thought was minor damage forward near the point of impact. Still, the concussion was so small it led him to think *Arctic*'s stout oak frames and thick pine planks remained intact. By the looks of the other vessel, *Arctic* was at least ten times the tonnage and more than one hundred feet longer. The difference in size of the two ships accounted for *Arctic*'s coming through the mishap relatively unscathed, Luce thought.

The yells drifting over the water from the Frenchmen moved Luce. He well understood their fear and could not help but feel compassion. Would not the French master come to his aid if their roles were reversed? It was a point of honor, an unwritten rule of the sea to help another vessel in distress, and what made the matter of even greater urgency was that he considered himself partly responsible for the harm *Arctic* had done to the other ship. The annals of seafaring history were full of heroic tales of one captain's coming to the rescue of another. It was a man's duty to do so—nothing less and nothing more. At that moment, Robert Gourlay and William Baalham emerged from the crowd, waiting for his orders.

"All slow ahead!" he called down to them, his voice calm. "Clear away the quarter boats, Mister Gourlay. We will circle round and render all possible assistance."

"All slow ahead, aye! Clear away quarter boats, aye!" Gourlay answered. He signaled the engine room to carry out the captain's orders, and the helmsman as well. Back in the wheelhouse, sweat trickled down the helmsman's back despite the chill in the air. He was trapped in a box without being able to see anything. But he knew there was danger, and his first thought was to run outside to see what was the matter. He could feel the tension in the air, but he stood by his post. He spun the wheel to begin making a tight turn to bring the ship around on a circular course.

"Mister Baalham, go with Mister Gourlay," Luce said. "We will send two boats to assist the Frenchmen."

"Aye, sir!" the second mate replied, and pushed his way through the throng of passengers and crew, which grew larger by the moment as nearly every soul aboard left their staterooms or duty stations to see what had caused all the commotion. They poured up through the companionways and out the doors of the saloons like the tide on a fast ebb in a narrow channel. Nothing could stop them. Although they showed no sign of panic, their excited voices made it difficult for Luce to shout above the noise to make his orders heard.

The ship's company gathered on the starboard side to watch the drama unfold, transfixed at the incredible scene playing out before them. Their combined weight caused *Arctic* to list slightly to starboard, serving as live ballast. This was common enough. Luce had seen the rush of immigrants aboard *Constellation* when she arrived in the upper bay, all intent on catching their first glimpse of New York City, tilt the big packet over as if she heeled to a fresh wind from abeam. Some captains locked the immigrants below until the ship was safe alongside in her berth to avoid the press of humanity and the confusion it created on deck. Luce did not condone this practice, nor did he think it necessary to lock people below to maintain the safety of his packet. The risk to the ship was small, and the people who had traveled so far in the hold of the packet ought to be allowed to rejoice at their moment of arrival in the New World. He noted *Arctic*'s list and attributed the ship's poor trim to the people, as he watched Gourlay set to launching the starboard quarter boat.

In moments, the starboard quarter boat was cleared, and two of the most important officers in charge of the sailing department, Gourlay and *Arctic*'s bosun, got in. Five sailors took their seats and unshipped the oars. Lowering a boat while the ship moved forward through the water required skill to avoid an accidental capsize. Gourlay's calm but firm voice reached the men on deck assisting with the launch. They listened carefully, ready to complete the maneuver. Down, down the boat went, until the men in it had to crane their necks to see their mates on deck. Whitewater seethed under the paddle wheel churning a short distance off the boat's bow and rushed astern. The ship's hull lifted and fell to the swells, at one time showing nothing but the sleek black surface of her topsides, the next green slime intermingled with white barnacles at the waterline and the oxidized copper sheathing below it.

"Easy boys! Easy now!" Gourlay called. "Ease her off. All ready forward, Mister Wilde?"

"All ready forward, aye," the bosun answered.

"Wait now, boys. Wait." Gourlay timed his next move with the motion of the ship and the rhythm of the sea. When a particularly large swell came up to meet the bottom of the boat, he cried out, "Cast off! Look lively there."

The turbulent water pushed the boat back hard against the hull. The men did not use their hands to push off. Well trained and well commanded, they resisted the impulse to shove off and possibly catch their hands and arms between the ship and the boat's side. The bow swung away on an eddy. The stern hit the ship again.

"Lay to the oars, boys! Put your backs into it!" Gourlay shouted, and they were at last free of the ship. People above watched them go, wondering what news they might bring back when they returned from the French steamer.

From his post on the paddle-wheel box, Luce sent orders to the helmsman to make his turn tighter, lest he lose sight of his men in the fog. The mist came in thick enough to obscure the French ship from time to time, only to have her loom surprisingly close when it cleared away a little. Frenchmen climbed the steamer's masts and inched out onto the yards, taking in sail. Others used axes to cut away the foremast. Gourlay's men rowed hard toward her, but he was still quite far away, and *Vesta* drifted fast to leeward. It would take him some time to reach her and get back, intercepting *Arctic* as she orbited the wreck. She lay dead in the water, beam to the swells. He could see her salmon-colored bottom when she rolled.

Luce noted that *Arctic*'s list appeared to increase and that her paddle wheel seemed to bite deeper than it should. He could tell by the sound it made as it turned. There was only a slight difference in pitch, but he had come to know it so well that he was able to tell approximately how many revolutions the wheel made per minute just by the sound of the water, the way the paddles slapped and churned, even the vibrations under his feet as he stood atop the paddle box. His ears were as finely tuned to the mechanics of the ship as they had been to the wind in the rigging of the packets he commanded. He grew uneasy. He hurried down the stairs of the paddle-wheel box and went aft just as Baalham lowered away the port quarter boat.

"Hoist that boat up again, Mister Baalham," he said, and motioned to the second mate to come to him. Baalham pushed his way through the crowd. "Go forward over the bow, Mister Baalham. Find out if she is holed, and if so, how badly."

"Aye, sir!" Baalham said, and made his way as quickly as possible toward the bow. As he forcefully cleared a path through the passengers, he observed the startled expressions on the faces of the ladies, and many of the men, as they saw him rush toward the bow. Baalham became increasingly worried. When he arrived at the bow, he saw several men struggling to look over the side, including one of the firemen, Dobbin Carnaghan.

From high up on deck, more than twenty feet above the waves breaking against the bow as the ship circled slowly around *Vesta*, it was not easy to discern the full extent of the damage. Carnaghan, a strong man used to the hard work at the furnaces below, could not contain his curiosity. With great effort, he "got partly over the side, to see what damage was done to us, and discovered the Frenchman's cutwater and bow sticking into us."

The sight of the big steamer literally impaled by the smaller vessel surprised and shocked Carnaghan. Minutes before he had just come off watch and was about to go to lunch. When the bell rang for all stop, then to back engines, "none of us in the engine room thought of a collision, nor we did not feel the slightest shock to indicate it." However insignificant the impact may have felt four decks down in the bowels of the ship, *Arctic* was indeed in danger. Carnaghan hurried below to see what he might do to assist his mates in the black gang.

With the help of some of the men standing nearby, Baalham also got partly over the bow to have a better look and "found three large holes in the ship, two below the water, one of which was about five and a half feet in length, and one or one and a half feet wide, leaving the whole cutwater and stem of the iron steamer clean through the Arctic's side."

Now Baalham understood the fear starting to ripple through the passengers. Several of the men, when they learned of the damage, told others, and word spread fast among the ship's company. He fought his way aft to tell Luce of his frightening discovery. Like all the other officers aboard *Arctic*, Baalham knew the six lifeboats could not take all the passengers, much less the crew. Although *Arctic* had the legal number of boats aboard for a ship of her size, no one thought to add more to accommodate every person who might sail in her at any given time. He had seen six years earlier what happened when panic spread through a ship, and he feared what might occur if it came time to take to the boats.

Just off Liverpool, while sailing aboard the packet *New World* in August 1848, Baalham had helped rescue men, women, and children from the Boston-based packet *Ocean Monarch*, which caught fire shortly after leaving port. The grisly scene replayed itself in his head by day and infiltrated his dreams at night for months and years afterward. The screams of the people burning alive as they leaped from the deck into the sea, causing the water to hiss and foam, haunted him. The smell was a terror to contemplate. Even now he sometimes thought he caught a whiff of burning flesh and hair on those warm, humid August days in New York when the weather was the same as it had been on that day off Liverpool. More than three hundred people had burned to death on *Ocean Monarch*, right before Baalham's eyes. For his part in the rescue of the handful of survivors, he was awarded a gold medal from the Massachusetts Humane Society.

There would be trouble on this day, he thought, as he raced up the stairs of the paddle-wheel box and reported his findings to Luce. The calm that had prevailed on deck began to disintegrate. Both captain and mate realized this. It was like a beast slowly awakened, dark and powerful, and unknown to all aboard but Baalham.

A shout came from forward; then an odd though temporary silence descended on the ship. People turned their attention away from the French steamer. They gathered together and stared as the first oily black jets surged from the outlets of the two Worthington steam pumps used to rid the bilges of water that routinely seeped in when the ship worked her seams in a seaway. Each outlet began discharging a solid column of water six inches in diameter. It stained the deck with slippery oil and gurgled out the scuppers over the side.

CHAPTER ELEVEN

DEADLY DAMAGE

Dnearly complete. Only faint smudges of light appeared, dimly visible as an opaque blue surrounded by the jagged tears in the ship's side.
The sea cascaded in through the holes around the sharp iron spikes of
Vesta's bow protruding into the hull, admitting thousands of gallons in
just a short time. The rats, resident on all vessels, scurried over the tops
of boxes and casks seeking escape as the water flowed aft and began to
rise on its inexorable way up to the level of the waterline nineteen feet
from the bottom of the keel. The shouts of men and the thud of axes
on the ceiling above the hold suddenly added to the noise. The water
rose fast. In just fifteen minutes, more than three feet of it covered
Arctic's bilges fore and aft.

A shadow passed over the holes, reducing the light coming
through them. The hold went almost dark for a few moments. The
flow of the water did not slow down. The shadow, caused when men on
deck tried to haul a sail over the holes, disappeared as the iron tore the
canvas to shreds. Several more attempts to secure other sails proved
equally unsuccessful. Passing a sail over a hole and tightening it with
lines led to the deck was an age-old measure to combat a bad leak. It
was common practice aboard ships of war when a cannon shot stove in
the hull, and it often worked. The incoming water forced the canvas
inward and although the material could not stop the flow entirely, it
bought precious time for the crews to reach the leak from the inside,
where more effective action to brace in a backing plate might succeed
in keeping the vessel afloat long enough to make port. But in *Arctic*'s

115

case, the remains of *Vesta* ensured that no hope existed for the temporary remedy to work.

Outside the hull, several feet above the holes at the water's surface, *Arctic*'s carpenter perched on a tiny raft of spars lashed together to form a platform. Waves broke over him while he used a pole to nudge mattresses and pillows down toward the openings, hoping to plug them. He strained and stretched to reach down far enough to wedge the bedding into the gaps, but each time he managed to get it close, the sea snatched it away. The bedding floated rapidly aft, and the paddle wheel ripped it apart. He kept trying, knowing that he must not fail. One of the ship's officers cried down to him that the water was already over the cargo, a sad discovery made when holes were eventually chopped through the ceiling of the lower hold in an effort to gain access to the leak. The forty-five-degree water hurt each time a wave covered him. He could not feel his fingers or toes, and he choked and gagged every time he went under. At last, he gave up, and crewmen hoisted him back aboard, wet and shivering, tired to the bone.

When the carpenter reached the deck, he saw an orderly sort of chaos. Francis Dorian, crewmen, and male passengers worked fast to move both of the ship's anchors over to the port side of the ship. They rigged block and tackle to drag the anchors across the deck, heaving and cursing as they tugged at the falls. Other men paid out the starboard anchor chain and let it run free until it hung down from the hawsehole. A sailor below inside the chain locker smashed free the pin holding it in place on a ring fixed to the hull. It hit the waves with a mighty splash and snaked under the ship as she moved slowly forward.

An experienced seaman, the carpenter knew his captain had ordered the weight shifted to counter the list to starboard. He glanced around and saw most of the passengers moving aft along the port side of the ship. Officers herded them like sheep to use their weight to improve the ship's trim. Empty water casks were lifted from the hold, filled with seawater, and rolled aft to add still more weight in hope of raising the bow high enough for yet another try at plugging the leaks.

Crew and passengers manned the four hand pumps and worked the handles with a will while others stood by to take over to relieve the exhausted men. They worked together in teams. Their muscles ached and stiffened from pain. Sweat poured down their faces and stained their clothing. The soft, clean hands of the male passengers soon blistered and bled, and even the strongest of the firemen could man the pumps for only a few minutes before they had to rest. The scene, however frenetic and in true keeping with a terrible situation being handled to the best of all abilities among the ship's crew, struck passenger James Smith as something less than orderly.

> I saw Captain Luce on the paddle-box, giving orders in one way and another, and most of the officers and men running here and there on the deck, getting into an evident state of alarm, without seeming to know what was to be done, or applying their energies to any one thing in particular, except in getting the anchors and other heavy articles over on to the port side of the ship. . . . Our ship seemed to right herself somewhat after getting the deck weight upon the larboard, but it was too evident that Captain Luce himself, as well as all hands, were becoming aware of our danger, and from the tremendous volume of water being thrown out from our steam pumps, I was convinced we were making water at a fearful rate.

Seeing that all his orders were being carried out properly and well, Captain Luce left his post on the paddle-wheel box and ran aft to Willie's cabin, worried that his son might panic from all the noise and confusion. He burst through the door, out of breath. Abraham Boydell was sitting next to the boy on the bed, holding the child's hand while quietly reassuring him. Boydell stood up when Luce entered the stateroom.

"I've already told Willie what has happened, Captain," Boydell said. "I'll stay with him."

Luce tasted fear, seeing his helpless boy in bed, his face pale, his lips trembling, and his eyes wide. His son would not have been exposed to this danger had he and his wife not thought a voyage might benefit him. The pathetic irony of the circumstances was not lost on Luce. He told Willie all would be well, though he knew in his heart that it would not.

Luce went to his child's side and squeezed his hand. There were many infants, children, and teenagers aboard the ship. His duty was to try to save them all, and as many of the men and women as he could. Some no doubt would die if the ship went down, and by now that seemed a foregone conclusion. But there were boats enough to seat all the women and children and most of the parents. It would be women and children first. He intended to ensure this unwritten law of the sea kept. He hurried back to his post.

Back on the paddle-wheel box, he raised his spyglass and squinted into the lens. Fog shrouded the ocean. The French steamer had vanished; perhaps she had already sunk. Out of the gloom, he caught sight of Robert Gourlay's boat. He took off his cap and motioned to him to return to the ship. He reached for the speaking trumpet kept close at hand on the paddle-wheel box and called to Gourlay. In a few moments, he saw the men straining at the oars pulling in *Arctic*'s direction. He shouted down to one of the officers on deck to put the liner on a course for Cape Race, about sixty miles away, and hoped Gourlay might intercept him now that he had changed the ship's heading.

Luce turned back to see Gourlay's men rowing hard, but the distance between *Arctic* and the lifeboat did not change in spite of the powerful strokes of the men at the oars. He wanted to order all stop to give his officer and friend time to catch up, but he did not. To do so would put the ship in even greater danger, costing him time he dared not waste. He could only hope that the brute strength of the sailors with Gourlay might overcome the odds against them.

J. W. Rogers had informed Luce that the water level was rising fast in the engine room, something he had figured out long before the engineer emerged from below blackened from the oil and grease in the bilgewater. With great difficulty, struggling in the deepening torrent, he and his crew managed to open most of the bilge injectors to allow the ship's engines to draw water for the boilers directly from the water rushing into the hold, rather than from the sea itself through intakes in the bottom of the hull. The boilers required 8,000 gallons of water per hour to drive *Arctic* at her maximum cruising speed. As long as the ship continued to move forward and the water did not reach the furnaces in the fire room, she could pump huge quantities of the flood from the bilge. Cape Race was a little over four hours away if he kept going. He could not stop for Gourlay. Yet he hesitated in ordering the engines to full ahead while there was still a chance for his first officer to make it back to the ship.

As he focused on Gourlay, the fog lifted enough to bring *Vesta* back into view. He heard a haunting wail, a keening that stabbed at his sense of conscience. He had no choice now but to make for land as fast as possible in a race against time, perhaps futile, but one he must attempt regardless of the outcome in his effort to save his ship and passengers. He could offer no assistance for the men aboard the little steamer his ship had struck with such devastating consequences. He grimly faced the reality that he had to leave them to die. He gripped the brass rails of the paddle-wheel box until his knuckles went white, and with all the will he had in him, he wished Gourlay's men would hurry.

James Smith caught sight of *Vesta* as *Arctic* steamed away, and like almost everyone aboard the liner he thought she was about to sink fast. Her bow buried itself even more deeply in the sea. Men crowded the deck in obvious panic and seemed to do nothing more to save themselves. Instead, those aboard *Vesta* screamed for help—from *Arctic*, and from God. As *Arctic* quickly disappeared in the fog headed for land, the cries of the Frenchmen further convinced Smith that the little steamer was doomed. "We merely passed her again, and she was in less than a minute hid in the fog, but scarcely out of sight, when we heard arise from her deck a loud and general wail of moaning and lamentations that told us of their burial en masse."

Unknown to all the souls aboard both ships at that moment, the men of *Vesta* would not die, while death awaited every woman and child aboard *Arctic* and all but twenty-two of her male passengers. Unseen from the deck of the liner as she steamed away were the valiant efforts of *Vesta*'s crew. Many of them ran below to brace the forward watertight compartment with spare spars, mattresses, sacks of flour, and other ship's stores, hoping the iron wall might withstand the force of the water rising against it. The bulkhead groaned under the weight of the sea, but it held back the flood that filled the forward part of the ship.

For more than a day the crew worked to keep *Vesta* afloat and ready her to get under way once again, then put her head toward the coast of Newfoundland, eventually reaching St. John's on September 30. Later, when the Frenchmen were asked about the collision, they reported hearing or seeing nothing more of *Arctic*. They assumed she made it safely to port and they spoke out against Luce for condemning them to what appeared to be certain death. Press reports commented that it was indeed a fateful decision for Captain Luce to have sped toward land, leaving the men of *Vesta* to their probable fate in an effort to save all the people aboard his ship. Had he stayed near *Vesta*, the majority of *Arctic*'s passengers and crew would have survived. The ship Luce had initially tried to aid but felt forced to abandon out of a sense of duty to his own vessel might have taken all of them aboard.

But Captain Luce responded to the moment-by-moment demands of the crisis, acting in what he thought were the best interests of the people in his charge. Like Smith, he saw *Vesta* merge with the fog and turned his attention to Gourlay as the first officer struggled to reach *Arctic*. The lifeboat appeared and disappeared in the fog. It was no use. Time had run out. Luce now faced a new painful and difficult decision, yet another that ensured the fate of so many of *Arctic*'s company. He concluded that he must order the engines to full ahead and leave Gourlay behind, the one man aboard ship whom the tough men of the sailing department were used to obeying without question. They had experienced little direct interaction with Luce. His position as captain put him above them in a godlike station issuing orders through his officers. Captains rarely spoke to their men directly, unless it was necessary to discipline them. Gourlay's absence in the hours to come was to severely limit Luce's ability to keep order as he tried in vain to save his command.

Luce raised the speaking trumpet again and shouted to Gourlay. The boat changed course and put her bow to the seas. Gourlay stood up, braced against the violent pitch of the boat, and strained to hear his captain.

"We must leave you on your own, Mister Gourlay!" Luce cried. "We must leave you!" Luce was not sure Gourlay had heard him. He wondered what the man must be thinking, but pushed the somber and disturbing thoughts from his mind. Gourlay's form began to merge with the fog. The boat slid into the trough of a large swell, and he and his men vanished from Luce's sight. Resigned to his decision, Luce called down to signal the engine room to make all speed full ahead. He turned his attention back to the commotion on deck, halfheartedly re-assuring himself that Gourlay was in a seaworthy boat with six strong men. Although they lacked provisions, it was possible they might find their way to land, or maybe luck might favor them with a ship passing close enough for the lookout to see them and initiate a rescue.

Arctic's paddle wheels beat faster and faster, reaching their average revolutions of fifteen turns per minute. The wake stretched out astern into a long band of slick water and white foam. The fog whirled past. The black smoke pouring from the stack streamed aft. The ship gathered way and plunged through the seas, her forward motion increasing the flow of water through the holes in the bow. Up forward, on the port side, several men began screaming. "Stop! Stop her!" Luce peered into the fog, but he saw nothing.

Out of the mist, the towering black shadow of the American

steamer suddenly appeared high above Jassonet François, like a night-mare repeated. The bow wave surged over the boat and nearly capsized it. The men rowed frantically to get out of the way. Some of them lost their grip on the oars. The enormous paddle wheel beat the water, pushing up a dark hump of seething ocean in front of it. It drew closer, closer. Several men jumped out of the rowboat, including Jassonet François, who sank beneath the icy waves. He heard the thump of the wheel as he was slammed against the hull, cutting his arms and legs on the sharp barnacles at the waterline before he was sucked under. All went dark for a moment. Water began to fill his lungs.

On *Arctic*'s deck, the crowd on the port side, which accounted for most of the female passengers, watched in horror as the wheel caught the boat and drove it under while smashing it into shards of wood. The men in it got caught in the floats, wedged in tight, as the wheel plunged them down more than seven feet below the surface. Their ag-onized wails pierced the air for only a second. The ladies turned away, shuddering and crying. Many of the men stood fixed in place, not be-lieving what they were seeing. The bodies of those in the boat rode the aft end of the wheel up under the paddle-wheel box, where the force and compression of the impact ripped their limbs and crushed their heads and torsos, freeing them from the floats. As they came down out of the front end of the paddle-wheel box, their broken bodies flew out-ward through the air and splashed into the sea. They were instantly driven under the wheel again and disappeared. It was as if they had never existed.

One of the onlookers, the young German sailor Ferdinand Keyn, took immediate action. Seeing that two or three men struggled in the water, with the paddle wheel gaining on them by the second, Keyn dashed to the side of the ship and grabbed a length of rope from the pin rail. He hurled the line overboard and shouted in German at the Frenchmen, pointing to the rope. The wheel crushed another and then another of the men in the water.

As Jassonet François shot to the surface, the wheel high above him, he heard Keyn screaming and looked up just in time to see the rope. He lunged for it. It was slippery, but he got hold of it, and immediately the forward motion of the ship dragged him under the water, filling his lungs again. He could not breathe but did not let go of the rope. He felt himself rising, slowly at first, then more rapidly. Summoning every bit of energy he had, his will to live tapping into the last reserves of his strength, he pulled himself up hand over hand, until he reached the bulwarks. Keyn and several others hauled him onto the deck, where he lay half-conscious, more dead than alive really, and vomited the sea from his stomach and lungs.

Passengers and crew looked up at Luce from the deck, true panic beginning to show for the first time. They yelled that *Arctic* had just crushed a lifeboat, that all in her had been killed save for one person. Luce nodded. He did not answer. He faced forward, his jaw set, a wild look of grief and anger on his face. William Baalham appeared a moment later. Luce ordered him below with any crewmen and male passengers he could muster to try yet again to reach the leak from the inside. Francis Dorian and two quartermasters also emerged from the crowd.

"Clear away the boats, Mister Dorian," Luce said. "The quartermasters will draw weapons and let no one near the boats until they receive orders from me."

"Aye, Captain," he said.

Down in the engine room, the water rose over the floor and threatened to extinguish the fires in the lower row of furnaces. Some of the coal heavers and firemen attempted to leave their posts, terrified that they might drown if the ship sank suddenly. J. W. Rogers, together with other officers, ordered the men to stand fast. Most of the men obeyed, though some ran up on deck, where they were met by First Assistant Engineer John Degnon on his way back below, after reporting the latest status of the ship to Captain Luce:

I then ordered—persuaded—several firemen and coal passers
to go below and keep the fires up, telling them that everything
depended on the pumps. On going below, I found the water

nearly to the grates of the lower furnaces. I went round and
opened the remainder of the bilge valves, (there being six in
all), in reaching down to them my face was under water.

Degnon held his breath as he worked the last of the bilge injectors
open with a heavy wrench. He had to get them all open to allow the engines to draw water directly from the bilge, buying the ship a little
more time to remain afloat. Again and again he plunged under the surface to emerge from the swiftly flowing water with a sputter, retching
from the oil he swallowed, his eyes burning. He had to keep them open
under the dirty water to accomplish his task. All around him in the fire
room, men worked passing coal from the bunkers to the firemen at the
furnaces. There were, however, fewer of them on duty than usual. The
exodus from the bowels of the ship had begun with the rats, then with
the members of the black gang.

CHAPTER TWELVE

BRAVERY TESTED

HEAVY SWELLS KICKED UP from the gale brewing near Cape Race rolled in over the Grand Banks with mounting strength. They did not yet exhibit the kind of awesome demonstration of the sea's power made clear from towering crests collapsing in thunder as their backs broke, unable to withstand the force of a screaming wind. These swells were more like low mountains topped with chop, a benign harbinger of the storm still well over the horizon. The ocean undulated and heaved, moving in its timeless rhythm, lifting the boxes, casks, and crates, mattresses, pillows, and sails to the summits to drop low in the troughs as the swells swept on to spend their energy against the precipitous bluffs of the Newfoundland coast. The trail of debris thrown overboard to lighten the ship or lost in efforts to slow her leaks stretched out for miles astern of *Arctic* while she raced toward land and the salvation for her people the shore represented.

The sea around the liner remained shrouded in dense fog that created a private little world in which the scenes on board played themselves out. The muffled boom of a cannon and the rapid clang of bells were all that announced her presence, signals ordered by the captain to alert any passing vessels of his ship's distress. But no vessels sailed near, despite the heavy traffic on the banks. No crews cocked their heads to listen intently for where the distress signals came from. *Arctic* steamed on alone, and every minute the water rose higher in her hold and her paddle wheels sank lower in the swells. Her speed dropped from thirteen knots to twelve, and steadily decreased until she began to wallow and roll.

At the bow of the ship was a group of two or three passengers assisting a young apprentice engineer, Stewart Holland. He rammed home the charges of black powder, made ready to fire, and shouted, "Stand clear!" The passengers stepped back and placed their hands over their ears. Holland touched the slow match smoldering in his right hand to the powder used to prime the charge. With a hiss and a white flare, it ignited the charge. Flames shot from the muzzle as the cannon roared and reared back against the tackle rigged to stop the recoil. Smoke blew aft across the deck. Soot and tiny burn marks covered his clothing and spotted the left side of his face. Every minute, Holland repeated the ritual. Ram the powder home, prime, and shoot. Ram, prime, shoot. The reports echoed and bounced off the walls of fog whirling around him. Droplets falling from the rigging sizzled when they hit the hot barrel of his cannon and disappeared in tiny puffs of steam.

Aft on the stern, stewards grabbed life preservers from lockers and gave them to the passengers gathered near the boats. There were two types. One consisted of a series of watertight tin cans held together with webbing to wear under the arms, and the other was a more modern invention—rubber rings that the wearers inflated like balloons. Men and women huffed and puffed to blow their life preservers up for themselves and for their children—only to stare in surprise, and then horror, as they slowly deflated. More than half of the rubber life preservers were not airtight and were therefore useless. In disgust, many of the passengers threw them overboard. Still convinced that *Arctic* might make the shore, that a vessel might come to their rescue, or that they might find a place in the boats, others refused to take either type of flotation device.

Among the latter were the Collins, Brown, and Allen families. James Brown and Edward Knight Collins owned *Arctic*. They were also good friends of the captain. William and Clara Brown, with their two-year-old daughter held close, stood with Grace Brown Allen, George Allen, and their infant. Millie Brown and William Gilbert and the

Collins family watched the increasing panic and huddled together aft near the boats, waiting for Luce to order them to get in, taking what they naturally felt were seats due them based on their lofty positions. Other important individuals expected the same treatment. All were to find that money and position counted for little on this day, but for the moment they remained oblivious.

Working in the dim, flickering light of oil lamps below, the men with Second Officer Baalham struggled to get at the leak. They swung their axes to cut away even larger portions of the ceiling, then pried apart the planks with iron bars. When the holes were large enough, the men peered into the black depths. Baalham lowered a lantern to light up the hold, which better revealed the mass of floating cargo. It banged and sloshed about from the ship's motion with enough force to make it almost suicidal to drop down inside, dive beneath the water, and drive wedges into the leaks to reduce the flow. Yet men tried to go in anyway, and some came dangerously close to dying in the hold. The roar of the water could be heard above the noise on deck. The boom of Holland's cannon, the ringing of the bells, and the weeping and shouting seemed far away, a dull hum of humanity set against the much louder rumble of the sea streaming in through the holes. Their best efforts at last spent, the men stood for a moment looking down into the hold, silently lost in the thought of what their failure meant for all aboard the liner.

A tremendous explosion of steam and smoke shook the lower decks. Frantic shouts and the sound of many men running from the fire room and engine room reached Baalham and those with him. Every man there knew that the inevitable had just occurred. The water had reached the level of the lower furnaces. As it poured in over the ash pits and red-hot grates, the coal burst and hissed in violent reaction. The doors flew open on their own as the water at the bases of the furnaces turned to steam in an instant. The upper furnaces remained lit, but soon they too would go out, the engines would stop, the Worthington steam pumps would sputter and die, and *Arctic* would lay helplessly in the trough until she sank.

Baalham sighed and dismissed the men. "It's no use," he said to them. "Up on deck with you, boys." Baalham went to check the status of the fires and the engines, hoping the pumps might be kept working for a little longer.

When Baalham arrived in the engine room, he found John Degnon nearly alone. A handful of firemen and one or two other officers stood fast to man the engines and keep the fires lit in the fire room, but almost everyone else had gone, including J. W. Rogers and his favored assistants. Every minute the fires burned in the upper furnaces meant additional miles made good toward land and more water pumped from the hold through the bilge injectors and the outlets of the steam pumps. Degnon refused to leave his post. He resolved to keep steam up as long as possible:

> The lower fires were all put out by the sea water. We then broke in the upper side bunkers; I passed the coal down to fire the upper furnaces. The steam [pressure in the boilers] at this time had fallen from eighteen to fourteen inches. I then took the working platform from Mr. Drown, junior first assistant engineer, being in the fire room, standing up to his waist in water.

At the moment the water hit the fires in the lower furnaces, billowing clouds of steam and black smoke poured from the vents on deck and wafted out of the hatches to merge with the fog astern. This confirmed to all those who witnessed it that the lower tier of furnaces had been extinguished. Luce felt the ship shudder. A few minutes later, he noted she slowed still more. The paddle wheel beneath his feet strained against the sea. It was not designed to dig so deeply, and the pressure on the iron fittings caused them to squeal and whine. Vibrations shook the platform. Now more than ever, Luce realized time had nearly run out for *Arctic*. She would never make it to land. "Finding the leak gaining on us very fast, notwithstanding all our very powerful efforts to keep her free, I resolved to get the boats ready, and as many ladies and children placed in them as possible," he reported later.

Luce pushed his way aft, where he found all in a state of panic. The crowd had overwhelmed the two quartermasters. Although they were armed, the weapons did not intimidate the people. Indeed, the quartermasters were as anxious as the rest to secure a place for themselves in the limited number of boats available. By this time most of the ship's company was all too aware that there were not enough boats to save everyone. He yelled as loud as he could that he wanted women and children to come to the boat on the port side. This boat was the one Baalham was launching just after Robert Gourlay had set off to assist *Vesta*. It was slung out over the side set to go.

Hearing Captain Luce's call for women and children, William Gilbert shepherded the ladies in his party through the crowd as fast as possible, trying to reach the boat: "I went [to the boat] with the ladies of my party, to endeavor to get them in. In going, however, Mrs. Allen inquired for her husband, saying that she could not go without him. The momentary delay caused by looking for him prevented us from being in time to get into that boat. When we approached, it was already filled."

Male passengers and crew fought to get in the boat Gilbert was trying to reach, but Luce and the quartermasters kept them back. Luce helped women and children take their seats, among them a pretty young lady, a Miss Smith, whom he assisted personally. He put the ship's butcher and one of the quartermasters in charge of the boat and her nearly thirty passengers. He saw to it they had provisions—a barrel of sea biscuits and a keg of water—and helped them lower away. The boat reached the water safely and tugged at the painter connecting it to the ship.

"Drop the boat astern," Luce said. "But don't cut loose from the ship!" He wanted to keep all the boats together and the officers he put in charge to make for land in convoy, there being safety in numbers.

Miss Smith suddenly realized that her father was not in the

lifeboat. She screamed for him and tried to jump overboard to regain the ship, just as the butcher, in defiance of Luce's orders, cut the painter and set the boat free. Men in the boat held Smith down. She kicked and scratched at them, wailing mournfully and calling for her father. A few moments later, the lifeboat disappeared in the fog. Smith's calls continued to reach the people on deck. Slowly they became less distinct, muffled in the moisture-laden air, until finally no one aboard *Arctic* heard them at all.

With the assistance of Francis Dorian and passengers, Luce prepared the second and last boat aft on the port side for launching under the protection of some crewmen still loyal to him and additional male passengers to hold back the crowd. Gilbert tried to reach this boat also, but he was too late once again. He could not get near it. A dozen women, some children, and several men, one of whom held an infant in his arms, took seats in the boat. The shouts behind Luce grew louder. A burly fireman, whom Luce recognized as Patrick Tobbin, burst through the line of passengers and tried to leap into the boat.

Tobbin had just come on deck from below, having abandoned his post in the fire room. In revealing detail, he described those few moments and his encounter with Captain Luce:

> Our only thoughts were now as to measures of escape. When I got on deck all was confusion; passengers were working with desperate energy at the forward pumps. Frenchmen, Germans, and English were all calling in their different languages to the firemen to help them, and running to and fro on the deck, sometimes rushing to the pumps, and rushing away again when relieved by others. . . .
>
> When I first attempted to leave [the ship], the captain caught me, and tore the shirt off my back to prevent my going, exclaiming, "Let the passengers go in the boat." He also seized a kind of ax [a heavy carpenter's mallet made of iron], and attempted to prevent the firemen reaching the boat; but it was

every one for himself, and no more attention was paid to the captain than to any other man on board. Life was as sweet to us as to others.

Captain Luce seemed like a man whose judgment was paralyzed. He paced the deck as if there was no resort but to sink with his ship. He could easily have saved himself had he sought his own safety.

As Luce fought with Tobbin, other firemen and sailors surged past him and the rest of those defending the boat. Male passengers joined them. They all scrambled to jump into it. He raced to the rail to block them, striking at the men trying to escape, and bellowed for them to stop. No one obeyed.

In the confusion, the forward tackle holding the boat ran free. The bow dropped fast and came up short when the falls jammed, flinging the women in backward somersaults over each other into the sea. Those who were not injured or knocked unconscious struggled to stay afloat, but their heavy clothing quickly soaked through and dragged them down. Of all the women in the boat, only one remained. She clung to the rope jammed in the bow tackle shrieking for her husband and infant, whom she saw sink together under *Arctic*'s hull. Passengers hauled her to the deck, where she promptly fainted. Two others survived, a male passenger and a steward. Both miraculously got wedged in between the seats as the boat fell.

The men in the water lasted longer than the women and children. Passengers looked on as they flailed and kicked desperately, thrashing in the ship's wake under the transom as she slowly steamed away. Corpses wearing the tin can life preservers joined the debris trailing off astern and rolled with the swells. Their arms and legs in death had found the rhythm of the sea and washed to and fro as if to embrace it.

Luce surveyed the mayhem he had tried to stop but could not, and rage bubbled up in a cool, calm fury. He found himself transformed from the jovial host, the dashing captain, the seasoned mariner, into something far baser. He was forced to become a brute. The crew and many of the male passengers knew no other way, respected nothing else. Reason, honor, and decency were alien to them. He angrily clutched the handle of the mallet and resolved to kill the next man to cross him. Choking back his emotions, he turned to Dorian: "We must save this boat, Mister Dorian. We have need of it."

Both men stood together and looked over the side. The boat hung at a forty-five-degree angle, its bow pointed down at a steep angle as the ship lumbered forward through the swells. Every time she rolled, the side of the boat smashed into the hull, threatening to wreck it.

"Aye, Captain," Dorian replied, his voice oddly quiet, the unsettling scene of death all around him having cut deep. "We will save her."

It would not be a simple matter to right the boat and hoist her up again, given the chaos and violence on deck and the motion of the ship as she rolled to the swells sweeping in off her stern. But there was always a solution. It was up to Luce to find one. Fast.

CHAPTER THIRTEEN

COWARDICE

WHEN WILLIAM BAALHAM emerged from below, the scene he witnessed struck him as all too familiar. No fires shot from the open hatches and roared out the doors and windows of the saloons. No flames licked the masts and yards or ignited the tar on the standing rigging to drip molten spheres down on the screaming passengers on deck, setting their clothing ablaze. Yet the similarity between the frenzied state of the passengers and crew aboard *Arctic* and those he had tried to rescue aboard *Ocean Monarch* remained striking in its palpable sense of hopelessness and despair. He stayed frozen at the companionway for a moment, taking it all in. He caught sight of Captain Luce and Francis Dorian near the empty davits aft on the port side of the ship. He stirred himself to action and raced to the captain.

"Captain Luce!" Baalham cried.

Luce whirled around, still clutching the iron mallet in his hand. Baalham's eyes darted to the weapon.

"The water is on a level with the lower deck beams, sir. It was impossible to get at the leak," Baalham said, his voice a bit strident and heavy with emotion. "Do you still think we can save her?"

Luce shook his head. "I believe she will soon sink, Mister Baalham. See to your boat. Drop her astern until we can pass women and children down to you."

"What are your intentions, sir?"

"The ship's fate will be mine," Luce said.

"What about your son? Shall I take him in the boat?"

"There are other people to be provided for, Mister Baalham. Willie will have to take his chances with me."

In the face of all that was happening, in spite of the natural desire of a parent to do anything to save his child, Captain Luce did not forget his honor. Baalham nodded grimly. He said, "I will see to my boat."

"Make it so, Mister Baalham, and see you bring her astern as quickly as possible."

Baalham quickly moved to the starboard side to clear away the last of the main lifeboats while Luce and Dorian turned their attention back to the boat dangling from its tackle on the port side. With the assistance of several crewmen, and others to keep the crowd back, he began to lower the boat away just as steam and smoke started flowing out of the vents and hatches again, indicating that the fires in the upper furnaces were going out one by one. The ship listed slightly to port and settled down by the stern because of the weight previously shifted away from the starboard side and because the passengers and crew mainly gathered aft along the port side of the liner watching the captain and third officer. Due to the list, the starboard fires might stay lit just a few more minutes. But that was all. It was less than two hours since the collision.

John Degnon, together with the last of the black gang, ran up from below, having just left his post a short time after Baalham had come to check the status in the engine room:

> He [Baalham] went on deck, and directly after the water washed the fires out, sending up through the hatches a heavy cloud of smoke and steam. The steam was then only one and a half pounds pressure. I then went . . . to the Captain and told him all our chances were lost with the pumps.
>
> I asked him if a sail could not be got over the leak. He replied: "It could not; for so much of the bow of the propeller [a propeller-driven ship, as opposed to a sidewheeler] stuck out from the side of our ship that it was impossible to get the

sail over it." The Captain then . . . endeavored to seat the passengers in the lifeboats. Most of them were crowded closely together on the port quarter of the ship.

I met Mr. Drown, the assistant engineer, on the upper deck, and proposed to him to get the men together to construct a raft. He would not agree with me, saying it would be of no use, as they [crew and passengers] would swamp it immediately. At this moment I heard Mr. Baalham's voice over the side of the ship giving orders. I looked over, and saw Mr. B., with five or six men, lowering the boat. The captain then stood on the upper deck superintending the same, and, as I thought, intended the boat for an especial purpose. I went out on the guard, and asked Mr. Baalham, "Shall I get into this boat?" He made no answer. I asked him a second time without receiving a reply. I was then convinced Mr. B. was acting under the orders of the captain, then on the upper deck. The act of lowering the boat was cool and deliberate. I opened the door of the [paddle-wheel box] and looked in, the [wheel] shaft then being three feet above water.

On turning round, I saw some fourteen or fifteen persons [jumping over the rails into] the boat. I then caught hold of the tackle which held the boat to the guard of the ship, to let myself down into the boat. Just as my feet touched the gunwale of the boat, the captain gave the order, "Drop that boat astern." The tackle was cut, letting me down backwards, when I was caught by the ankle by Mr. Baalham and another, who drew me into the boat.

Captain Luce ran to the starboard rail in time to hail Baalham and repeat his orders to drop the boat astern and keep close to pick up women and children. There were three lifeboats left aboard, and one of them, the last of the steamship's largest boats, hung suspended at a precipitous angle after the capsize that pitched dozens of passengers into the freezing water. The ship still steamed slowly forward on her last bit of power. The confusion on deck had reached the point of anarchy:

> The same fearful scene [occurred] as when the first boat was being launched—men leaping from the top of the rail twenty feet, crushing and maiming those who were in the boat. I [Luce] then gave orders to the second officer to let go, and row after the ship, keeping under or near the stern, to be ready to take on board ladies and children, as soon as the fires were [completely] out and the engines stopped. My attention was then drawn to the other quarter boat . . . hanging by one tackle.

Baalham and those with him did not row after *Arctic* to stand "ready to take on ladies and children," though their boat was not filled to capacity even after picking up two or three other men struggling in the water. Instead, according to John Degnon, they "drifted out of sight of the ship" into the fog. The boom of Stewart Holland's cannon carried far and could have been used to find their way back to the steamer. For a time, the reports of the gun connected them to the ship they had just deserted in an auditory sense alone. They listened for a while, but eventually began their long row to Newfoundland. All save one in the boat were crewmen; there were no women or children in her.

These men, along with the others still aboard *Arctic* seeking to save their lives instead of working to rescue as many passengers as possible, acted in direct violation of one of the most important laws of the sea. For centuries, captains and crews adhered to the honorable tradition that unequivocally gave women and children the right to go first to the boats. There were indeed instances of barbaric acts among sailors regarding the passengers in their charge, but these cases remained rare on well-disciplined ships such as those engaged in the Collins Line.

The men also acted in direct violation of the laws of the United

States. In 1842, in the case of *United States v. Alexander Holmes* argued in the Circuit Court of Philadelphia, precedent was set to ensure sailors knew their duty and would carry it out or suffer the legal consequences. The court ruled that in the event of shipwreck or "extreme danger," sailors were required to "sacrifice their lives" in the line of duty for the benefit of passengers. It stated that under no circumstances was a sailor justified to condemn passengers to death to save his own life, nor was he justified to remove passengers from wreckage for the same purpose.

The law was clear, as was the moral duty that laws can never do more than mandate. Nevertheless, a large percentage of the crew flagrantly disregarded the fact that they were honor bound to do their duty. They resorted to a level of cowardice that would bring shame and dishonor to every member of the U.S. merchant marine and cause much finger-pointing in Europe about the brash and brutal nature of Americans in general—arrogant, self-serving, and lacking in their ability to uphold the standards of the Old World.

Captain Luce did not know yet that Baalham had abandoned him. However, he did realize Baalham's boat had momentarily gone out of sight. It was reasonable to assume the second officer had dropped beyond the stern into the fog, but was standing by to give aid to the passengers when the ship stopped moving. Luce focused all his energy on saving the last of *Arctic*'s largest lifeboats still available for women and children. He and Dorian gathered several men whom they trusted to right the boat and hoist her back up to enable the passengers to get in. The remaining quartermaster, a strong, wiry man long accustomed to working on sailing ships high aloft in the rigging, volunteered to go down to the boat.

He stepped out over the side of the ship, struggling to keep his balance as she rolled. With only the strength in his arms to support him, he grabbed the davit and, hanging and swinging from it, worked his way hand over hand out to the end. When he reached the ropes taut from the tension and weight of the boat more than fifteen feet below him, he clasped his feet firmly against the line and lowered himself down as he had done many times before when tarring the stays and shrouds of a full-rigged ship. The boat plunged and crashed against the liner's hull. Carefully he climbed into it, crawled forward, and grabbed the painter. The next move was even more important: he had to pass the painter up to the men on deck to allow them to haul the boat back up to deck level on an even keel.

Above him on the guard, Dorian and Luce waited for the right moment. As the boat rose on the back of a large swell, the quartermaster stood up and heaved the painter to them. Dorian lunged for the rope, leaning precariously over the side, and just barely managed to catch it. Together with his captain, they waited for the quartermaster to climb back out of the boat. When he was safely aboard, they again waited. All the men held fast to the rope.

"Easy, boys!" Luce called. "Easy. Wait for her to lurch."

Luce intended to use the ship's motion to help haul the heavy boat upright. As *Arctic* rolled, they took up the slack on the line. "Haul short, boys! Heave!" he yelled. The liner rolled back the other way, and the full weight of the boat yanked at the rope. Their muscles strained to keep up the tension on the line. Again and again, they repeated the process, until the boat was upright and high enough to make the painter fast, and get the boat back to a level just below the bulwarks, ready for loading.

As they were preparing the boat to take on passengers, William Gilbert forced his way through the crowd and called to Luce. "Can you let us have seats in this boat to save my friends?"

"Yes, bring them this way," Luce said.

Gilbert rushed away to gather the ladies and gentlemen of his party. "Captain Luce says we can go in the boat!" he said. "We must hurry."

Gilbert grabbed Millie Brown by the hand and told her all would be well at last. Together, the couple ran for the boat in the company of Clara and William Brown, with their daughter, Grace, and George

Allen, and their infant, and several others. They looked briefly for the Collins family but did not find them in time. When the party reached the boat, they found Luce screaming madly at two firemen who had jumped in.

"Get out now!" Luce yelled. "Get out!"

The two men, black with coal dust and soaked in seawater and sweat, reared up in the seats. "We will not!" one of them shouted back. "Our lives are as good as theirs!" He drew a knife and threatened Luce with it.

"Get out now, or I will kill you both!" Luce said, his voice suddenly quiet, his face taut with rage. He raised the iron mallet. "I will kill you."

The man with the knife froze. He stared hard at the captain. Gilbert saw cold and cruel hatred.

Luce raised the mallet higher over the heads of the firemen. From his position, he could easily have killed them.

Slowly, without saying another word, the men got out of the boat.

"Now get in," Luce said to Gilbert and the rest of them.

Gilbert jumped into the boat and cried, "Pass the ladies down to me!"

Before Luce could stop them, a rush of sailors, firemen, and male passengers beat him aside. The ladies screamed. Many were knocked to the deck and trampled. Others managed to get out of the way. The men surrounded Luce. Again, he could easily have killed several of them. All he had to do was swing his mallet, and men would die, their skulls crushed with one blow. But he did nothing. He could not bring himself to kill. Helpless, he watched the men leap over the rail.

Many of the male passengers fought with the crew to secure a place for themselves in the boat before it was lowered away and set adrift, filled to capacity with men. The boat reached the water, amid the rain of human beings. The young French duke, duc de Gramont, as he was called, teetered on the rail for a moment, then dove head first over the side. The cold water engulfed him and took his breath away. Above him, his manservant, Dulaquais, saw his employer struggle and knew that he was on the verge of drowning. He threw the duke a rope and hauled him aboard. Seeing the duke was safe, Dulaquais jumped for the boat himself and landed on top of those already embarked. He cried for the duke to try again. Shaken and numb from the frigid ocean, Gramont hesitated. He thought better of joining the mass of live bodies churning the water below and fatefully decided to take his chances on *Arctic*.

One of the more agile and crafty jumpers was Charles Mitchell, the cotton merchant from South Carolina whose sister had awakened in her bed in Liverpool to a premonition of evil. Her presentiment, it seemed to Mitchell, had proven all too accurate. He grabbed hold of one of the braces, lines used to control the square sails. He paid out enough slack to allow him to swing down to the boat like a trapeze artist in a circus. In a wide arc, he swooped far from the ship's side and landed right in the boat as it banged and crashed against the liner's hull.

William Gilbert looked on in horror at the scene as he drifted away with the others and eventually met up with Baalham's boat before proceeding to Newfoundland in company. He, like the rest of them, was overjoyed at having found a place in the boat that might well mean the difference between life and death:

> As I was carried away from the ship, I saw Mr. Edward Sanford standing on the saloon deck. He saw me in the boat, and with a smile on his face, waved his hand to me as quietly as if we were about to leave him for a short excursion. Mr. Brown I saw standing on the guard aft of the wheel-house. He bowed his head to me, but I did not hear him speak. I told him, in brief terms, my agony at having failed in my efforts to assist his party.

This, the last of the largest boats, disappeared like the rest into the fog.

Now the engines stopped working below. The paddle wheels stopped turning. *Arctic* lost momentum, and she stopped. Soon she lay beam to the swells, rolling violently.

It was then that Luce learned Baalham had truly deserted the ship, that he was not holding station nearby. It was then that Luce also learned that while he fought to save the passengers aft, his chief engineer, J. W. Rogers, along with his assistants, armed with pistols and carrying ample provisions, including cigars, had gone forward and stolen one of the two boats remaining aboard the liner. They left with the boat only half full and threatened to shoot anyone who came near. *Arctic*'s last boat was not big enough to take more than thirty passengers, and she would be well overloaded at that.

"When I reported to Captain Luce that all connected with the sailing department had left he gave a sort of despairing exclamation, and then with his sanction the passengers and myself proceeded to get our spars overboard to form a raft," Dorian said.

Luce's battle to save *Arctic*'s people appeared to have ended even before she sank beneath the waves.

CHAPTER FOURTEEN

FINAL MOMENTS

THE MIDAFTERNOON SUN failed to burn through the thick layer of
fog blowing eastward on the heels of the wind coming off the land
approximately forty-five miles away from the liner, but the sunlight did
penetrate the mist. It created a world of white and gray around *Arctic*,
almost beautiful in the way the vapor appeared to cradle the ship as she
tossed on the sea. It made diamonds of the droplets of water beaded on
the spars, deckhouses, and the brass rails along the promenade deck,
and painted shining streaks down the sides of the hull that glittered in
dull sweeps across her black, smooth planks. High in the sky, when the
light hit the tiny particles of water suspended in the air, the atmosphere
seemed to sparkle in an array of pinks, blues, and greens, a rainbow
without form, a spectacle of nature wonderful and grand.

As the afternoon passed, the sunlight diminished, and the ship
began to merge with the darkness gathering to the east. She presented
less of a profile than she had even an hour or two earlier. Her hull no
longer rose up like a cliff from the surface of the ocean. The bold, blunt
cut of her bow inclined toward the deepening gray of the heavens, and
her stern sank low to the waves breaking against her. She assumed her
final trim. The water that had once sunk her by the bow in those first
moments after the collision now flowed in and ran aft because of the
combined weight of the passengers and crew gathered on the upper
deck, the highest position above the sea.

Although *Arctic* was one of the largest ships in the world in the
1850s, she was small by modern standards, and as such her trim could
be changed simply by shifting people from side to side or from bow to

stern. In an effort to raise the bow early on, the passengers were ordered aft and to port. The liner responded, settling onto an even keel as she dashed toward land. As the water rose, with the passengers still aft and mostly on the port side, she began listing to port and going down by the stern in spite of being holed forward. Her human cargo through sheer numbers managed to defy the ship's natural tendency to sink bow first. Now, with her time short, the sea within her forced her transom lower every minute and began to raise the gaping holes in her bow closer to the surface within reach of a capable crew aboard a raft. But it was too late for any repairs to be effective, and there were no skilled men willing or able to try to make them. In less than an hour, *Arctic* would enter a void where sunlight was unknown and come to her final berth atop the mud and sand of the Grand Banks.

Already broken and beyond hope of salvage, *Arctic* underwent one last transformation from the splendid steamship she had once been to the wreck she would soon become. The people aboard her, desperate not to join her on her descent to the bottom, set about ripping her apart piece by piece to build themselves rafts on which to escape from the sea's call. They climbed the mainmast, and with the help of their captain and his only remaining officer, who showed them how, they removed her yards. Passenger Ferdinand Keyn, one of the last experienced sailors aboard, offered his help. There was at least one other sailor, a sea captain, who also helped Luce and Dorian. But all of the sailors in *Arctic*'s crew had left in the boats. Even the carpenter who had bravely tried to stop the leaks deserted the ship almost two hours before she sank.

The largest of the spars on the mainmast weighed almost a ton. Men on deck, unaccustomed to the work of the sailor, strained against the halyards, cursing and crying from the pain in their backs, shoulders, arms, and hands as they lowered the yards one by one to form the backbone of the raft. Other men hefted the yards up over the side of the ship and launched them overboard, along with sofas, settees, gratings, hatch covers, empty water casks, and anything else that might float and possibly save a life. Still others ripped doors from their hinges and planks from the deckhouses, and piled them on deck in preparation for lashing the pieces together. This process took more than two hours, and every minute the ship sank lower by the stern.

While some of the men worked together, many more abandoned all hope. They drained the bar dry, drinking bottle after bottle of hard liquor, and when that ran out, they smashed the locks on the storage closets containing the rest of the supply. They passed out on deck. The half-empty bottles in their hands rolled away and sent the contents pouring out the scuppers. They menaced the women in a last wanton attempt to gratify their lust in the time left before the ship sank and were chased away by the gentlemen protecting their mothers, wives, daughters, sisters, and aunts.

Still others bided their time. Like carnivores scenting blood, they watched Francis Dorian launch the last boat, taking care to remove the oars and the thole pins needed to keep them in place to discourage any who might try to steal the boat and make away with her. They watched him, together with several other men who volunteered to help, bring the boat around to the side of the ship to use as a working platform in an effort to lash the pieces of the raft together. They coldly observed their captain as he formed a barrier with a few men to keep back the crowd that threatened to delay the construction of the raft and went below to check on the level of the rising water. Among this group was Patrick Tobbin. He did nothing to assist the captain or third mate. Like the others, he waited for his chance. He knew it would not be long in coming.

Captain Luce made his way quickly below, fearing what might happen topsides in his absence. He found Professor Reed and Miss Bronson seated in a passage, quietly comforting each other. He left them, saying he thought the time was now short for them all. The cabins were mostly empty. Small groups of men and women scared to encounter the crewmen on deck cowered in their staterooms. Many refused to leave, and Luce did not spend much time trying to persuade them. After all, he thought, it made little difference where a person was when a ship sank. The suction caused when the vessel plunged deep would draw anything in the vicinity down with it. The end might come faster for those in the cabins. There was something merciful in that, and he left them to face their deaths in privacy.

Luce heard a pump working steadily. The sound surprised him, and he went forward to investigate. There was a stewardess, one of the two aboard hired to tend to the needs of the lady passengers, straining mightily to move the handle. Blood dripped from her dark brown hands and ran down the length of the pump handle, splattering her dress and staining her shoes.

"Come up on deck, Miss Downer," he said softly to her. "You're only exhausting yourself. It's as useless for you to try to pump out the ship as it is to pump out the ocean."

Without pausing, Downer said, "Captain, I'm willing to pump as long as I can work my arms."

"It's no use, Anna," he said. This lady, a servant to all those fine women of wealth, one of the lowliest members of the crew, standing fast while so many of the big, strong crewmen fled, was a sight that Luce would later describe in detail.

"Can you take me with you in the last boat, Captain?"

"I will not be going," Luce said. "When the ship sinks, I will be with her." Luce placed his hand on her shoulder and told her to go on deck. She hesitated, but seeing he was right, she left her self-imposed duty at the pump.

Luce proceeded farther below and found the water rushing and swirling like a great river running aft through *Arctic.* He went back up on deck and rushed aft to the uppermost level of the ship atop the deckhouses, where he found Willie with Abraham Boydell. He said a few words of comfort to Willie, ensured that the tin can life preserver Boydell had found for him fit snug and tight, and told the passengers that the raft would soon be ready and to try to keep calm.

Luce noted that the Brown, Allen, and Collins families stood together, gathered in prayer. They all looked remarkably calm, accepting their probable fate in a civilized manner. The ladies in particular "exhibited the most admirable coolness, and stared death in the face with a heroism which should have put to the blush the men who deserted and left them to their fate," Dorian said. Henry Coit Collins had removed his boots and coat, thinking correctly that they might encumber him when he hit the water. Although he was offered a life preserver, he refused to take it "while there was even one lady aboard without one." Luce saw a male passenger, an expressman from Adams & Company who was carrying important papers to Washington, helping to strap a life preserver on Mrs. Collins. Her daughter already wore one. The children clung to their parents, and many, including his son, were crying and shaking with fear.

A young physician approached Luce and shook his hand warmly, saying he knew his captain had done all he could to save the ship. The doctor pointed toward the bow, where Stewart Holland still manned his gun, now all alone. "Captain," he said, "should you ever live to reach the land, let the world know that here's one man who has done his duty bravely."

Luce nodded. "I know it," he said, "for I have seen him throughout." Other passengers approached him, crowding around. He again reassured them, though he knew there was no way all of them could get on the raft or in the boat now in Dorian's charge. He suspected they knew it too. He pushed his way through the men milling on deck back to the line of volunteers keeping the mob away from the side of the ship, and the forty-foot raft taking shape below.

The spars ground against each other and splintered as the ship rolled. The men working with Dorian tried desperately to avoid being crushed while tightening the lashings. Waves swept over them and more often than not, they worked up to their necks in the freezing water, ducking under the raft now and then to pass lines up between the crevices and through the cracks. How many might the raft hold? Luce wondered. How many might live to see tomorrow?

One man, second-class passenger James Smith, had already found a lucky means of escape, and because of his luck, he stood a fine chance for survival. For the moment he was safe, and he acted as a witness instead of a direct participant in the disturbing events that led up to the time just before *Arctic* sank:

The engines had stopped working, and I, seeing that the Chief Engineer, with some of his assistants and firemen had got the forward boat in the water over by the bow, under the pretence I saw of working at the canvas, which was hanging over the bow, so as to sink it down over the leaking places; but seeing, as I thought, symptoms of their real intention to get off from the ship, without too many in the boat, I dropped myself down nearby them on to a small raft of three planks about a foot wide each, and ten or twelve feet long and an inch in thickness, lashed together with some rope and four handspikes. . . . [This was the raft initially launched to use as a platform for the carpenter to work on just after the collision.]

Finding it bore me up [he could not sit down, though] I shoved off, intending to get alongside of the engineer's boat, but as I shoved off several firemen and one or two passengers dropped down into the boat, the engineer protesting against their doing so, and at the same time pushed off and pulled well away from the ship, with about twelve or fourteen persons in the boat, declaring to those on board, at the same time, that he was not going off, but would stay by the ship to the last. At the same time, he or those in the boat with him, continued to pull away in what I considered was the direction of the land, and were in a few minutes lost in the fog.

I now saw there was no probable chance for me but to remain where I was, on my frail little raft, until I could see some better chance after or before the ship went down. She had now settled down to the wheelhouses. The upper furnaces had for

ARCTIC UNDER SAIL

Arctic, the most luxurious steamship of the Collins Line, was known as
the "clipper of the seas" under her proud captain, James C. Luce.

Edward Knight Collins, manager of the United States Mail Steamship Company, commonly known as the Collins Line. His wife and two children died in the shipwreck.

EDWARD KNIGHT COLLINS

Samuel Cunard, founder of the Cunard Company of Great Britain, the chief rival of the American Collins Line. Most of Cunard's liners were engaged in carrying British troops to the Crimea in 1854 when Edward Knight Collins suffered "The Great Disaster."

SAMUEL CUNARD

SIDE-LEVER STEAM ENGINE

One of the fastest ocean liners in the world in the mid-1850s, *Arctic* cruised at more than thirteen knots. The nearly two-story-high side-lever steam engine shown here is similar to her twin 1,000-horsepower engines.

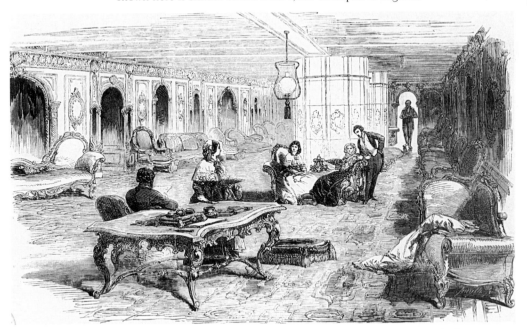

GRAND SALOON

Coupled with the latest in engineering, the Collins Line offered its pampered passengers the comforts of the Grand Tour's finest hotels. This is a view of the Grand Saloon of *Arctic's* sister ship *Atlantic*.

Arctic gets under way from her dock at the foot of Canal Street in Manhattan. One of the figures standing on the massive paddle-wheel housing is Captain Luce. Luce would later survive the shipwreck by clinging to this housing after it became mere flotsam.

ARCTIC LEAVING THE DOCK

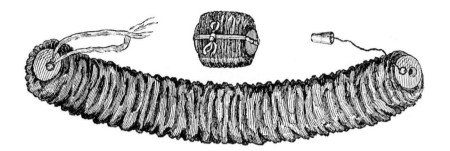

AN INFLATABLE LIFE PRESERVER THAT DID NOT WORK

The life preserver shown here is similar to some of those carried on *Arctic*.
They were made of a series of inflatable rubber rings that leaked and were thus
useless. The other type of life preservers consisted of a series of airtight
tin cans lashed together. These proved more effective.

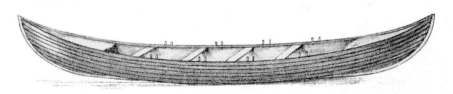

THE LIFEBOATS THE *ARCTIC* CARRIED

This is an example of a Francis metal lifeboat. *Arctic* carried six of them,
but there were not enough seats for all those aboard the liner.

PACIFIC RESCUES JESSE STEVENS

Arctic's sister ship *Pacific* rescued the crew of *Jesse Stevens* (behind and to the right) in 1852. Two years later, the captain of *Jesse Stevens* would save the life of Captain Luce.

STEWART HOLLAND

Stewart Holland is fancifully depicted here, but he was one of the few crewmen to remain solidly loyal. He bravely continued to fire the signal gun in the hope that a passing vessel might hear—until a wave engulfed him.

CAPTAIN LUCE AND WILLIE

Captain Luce and his son Willie did not remain in the fray on deck, as shown here, but retired to the paddle-wheel box, where they could await their fate together and alone.

ARCTIC SINKING
N. CURRIER

On September 27, 1854, *Arctic* struck another steamship off Cape Race, Newfoundland, in dense fog. *Arctic* sank in five hours of sickening tension turning to savage panic. Of the eighty-seven men rescued, only twenty-two were passengers. Not a woman or child survived.

some time been drowned out. People on board were doing nothing but firing signal guns of distress, trying to get spars overboard, and tearing doors off the hinges. Nothing else seemed to present itself as a means of saving the lives of some three hundred souls still on board. I have crossed the Atlantic nine times now, and nearly every previous time have had in charge one or more of my family or near relatives, but now I thanked my God that I had not even an acquaintance with me in this my adversity. . . .

I tightened up my little raft as well as I could so as to withstand the buffetings and strainings of the heavy rolling sea, and with the aid of a long narrow piece of plank which I tore off the others, using it as a paddle, I kept hovering within about 200 or 300 yards of the sinking ship. . . . In this position I saw three different small rafts like my own leave the ship, one of them with three and another with two of the firemen standing erect on them, the third with the old Frenchman [Jassonet François] we had already picked up, and one of the mess boys of the ship sitting on it.

I noticed, also, a couple of large empty water casks lashed together with five men on them, apparently passengers, leave the ship, and drifting towards me; while within about fifty yards they capsized with the force of a heavy swell, giving their living freight an almost immediate watery grave. Three of them, I noticed regained the top side of the casks only to be immediately turned over again, and the casks separating I saw no more of them. My heart sickened at so much of immediate death, and still I almost longed to have been one of them.

The large raft under construction was not yet finished when the ship settled quickly down, as if she had fallen off a ledge. Instantly, cries rent the air: "She's going! She's going!" That was all the men needed to hear. They again rushed Luce and his few companions. They

149

forced him aside and leaped over the rails, landing en masse on the raft. They scrambled across it, crushing the hands and fingers of the men in the water trying to secure the lashings, and clambered into the boat. Dorian had placed a crewman at the bow armed with an ax. He swung wildly and beat and bashed the men near him, but they did not concern themselves with the possibility of being decapitated or suffering other wounds from the blows of the axman. They went wild with terror:

> A perfect mania seemed to seize all on board and a universal rush was made for the boat, so that no possible entreaty or threat could stop it. The boat was perfectly crowded, and in order to save it from being swamped I [Dorian] ordered the painter to be cut and shoved clear of the raft, when I went about half a boats length from the raft, they were seizing everything afloat to endeavor to reach the boat. I ordered the people in the boat to make every effort to keep her from drifting off, at the same time I hailed Captain Luce, "For God's sake, Captain. Clear the raft so we can work! I won't desert the ship while there is a timber above water."

Luce stood motionless, silent in his anger and grief. The men who fought beside him to keep the crowd back had all disappeared over the ship's side with the rest, and some of the women jumped as well. He stood amid the milling swarm of humanity on the deck, despairing over all that had occurred and feeling responsible for it. He was barely able to talk, and at that moment, he was the loneliest man aboard *Arctic*.

The water around the raft teemed white with the thrashing of human beings, like a school of fish flipping in a net as they tried to reach the boat. Some of the stronger men, including Patrick Tobbin, managed to get to Dorian and were hauled aboard. Women drowned or were forced under the waves by the men struggling for their own lives. The raft was not yet fit for carrying a large freight of people. The lashings were not tight enough to stop the spars from working them loose in the swells. Looking down at the raft, Luce saw it covered with a writhing mass of bodies.

Arctic lurched again, this time with a more pronounced dip astern. Luce turned away from the carnage in the water, the vain battle for life that would soon end when the ship sank and pulled all who were not on the raft or aboard Dorian's boat far down into the dark embrace of the North Atlantic. His duty was not yet done. He grabbed a bundle of life preservers, rushed to the upper deck, and helped as many women put them on as he could in the last minutes that his command remained afloat.

Passengers gathered around Luce. Some of them wept; others remained stoically resigned to their approaching deaths or were unable to move, propelled into an almost catatonic state brought on by scenes witnessed during the past four hours. The Brown, Allen, and Collins families all wished Luce well and went off by themselves to wait for the inevitable time when the sea would separate them from each other forever. Captain Pratt, his wife, and their child were also on the upper deck, all too aware of the sad irony of having been so recently rescued from their foundering ship only to find themselves once again at the mercy of the sea.

Men and women, all dressed in their fine clothes and heavy overcoats, came to Luce to shake his hand, with evident affection, and to wish him good-bye. "Farewell, my good Captain," said Mrs. Childe, a wealthy and kind-hearted woman from Massachusetts, whom Luce had gotten to know during the voyage. Her daughter, one of the most beautiful ladies aboard the ship, bowed her head and cried.

Mrs. Hudson approached him with her young boy. With tears streaming down her face, she asked, "Captain, can we come with you in the boat?"

"It is not possible for you to go," Luce said.

It was not possible for any of them to go. It was too late. The collision had set in motion a chain of events that ensured these men and women, as well as their teenagers, children, and infants, would never again admire the blazing fall foliage soon to be dressing the environs of New York in a spectrum of orange, red, and yellow even more intense in color than when *Arctic* set off on her last voyage earlier in September. They would know no more the promise and pain of life. It was done.

Luce made his way to Willie and lifted him up in his arms. He rocked him to and fro.

Abraham Boydell shook Luce's hand and wished him farewell. "You don't have a life preserver," Boydell said to his friend and employer. "Take mine." He began to unstrap it.

Luce reached out and put his hand over Boydell's to stop him. "You will have need of it, Abraham," he said. "You had better keep it."

Luce left the passengers gathered on the upper deck, now separated into small groups consisting of family and friends. Some passengers without companions stood apart from the rest and stared aft at the water starting to rise over the stern, facing death alone. Wives and husbands and all the others would grieve for them when the news of *Arctic*'s loss reached home.

The ship angled downward. She assumed an incline of five degrees to the stern, ten, fifteen, twenty, and gradually the water covered the lower portion of the transom. Luce hurried forward. He ran down the stairs of the upper deck, carrying Willie and whispering words of comfort to him. He glanced aft. The water rose over the top of the bulwarks and started to roar. He heard the cabins filling in a cacophony of crashes—breaking glass and splintering wood as the ship's once opulent interior tore apart.

Luce climbed the stairs of the starboard paddle-wheel box and let his son down beside him. Willie leaned against Luce for support and buried his head in his father's heavy pea coat. They stood together hand in hand at the aft end of the platform pinned to the brass rail because of the steepening incline of the steamer. With a rush of escaping air from below, *Arctic* began her steady and final plunge into the sea.

CHAPTER FIFTEEN

DEATH'S COLD GRASP

THE SEA SWEPT OVER *ARCTIC'S* stern in a maelstrom of dark water and white foam. It rumbled and roared on either side of the ship as her bow eased skyward. There was no quick incline to an almost vertical position, no massive lunge to find the bottom. She slowly backed into the waves at a twenty-five-degree angle, assuming grace and beauty even in her last moments. The swells rolled over the aft deck and reached the upper deck where the passengers stood. The sea churned on three sides of the deckhouse level to the passengers' feet. It surged astern and to port and starboard, and closed in like the rising tide on a sandbar that submerged at high water. Up forward, Stewart Holland rammed the last charge of black powder down the muzzle of the signal cannon, racing against time. He had less than a minute before the water reached him at the bow.

Arctic sank more quickly now, gathering momentum and setting loose the power of the ocean to sweep her decks clean of all who were still aboard. As she slipped below the swells, the raft the few had struggled to build to save as many passengers as possible jammed under the paddle-wheel box and crushed several people who were on it, killing them instantly. Pieces of the raft ripped apart and toppled most of the rest still clinging to it into the water. Down it went with the ship, until what was left shot out from under the hull and bobbed in the swells.

The water rose higher. The waves on each side of the upper deck met in a furious rush just as Holland touched the slow match to the powder used to prime his cannon. The report exploded over the water as the waves lifted the passengers off their feet and hurled them in a tangled mass of bodies into the smokestack. Holland watched the waves carrying the dying men, women, and children toward him, his face burned black from the smoldering powder, his clothing wet from the fog and his sweat. In seconds, the crests rose up above his head and launched him over the bow.

Their oars still aboard the liner, the men in Francis Dorian's boat used bits of plank, the heads of axes, and their hands to paddle away from her as she went down. They feared she might suck the boat into the depths. They paddled hard and in silence. Patrick Tobbin put his back into his work, but he could not help looking upon the scene with morbid fascination:

> Just before we pushed off to avoid being carried down with the ship, I saw a number of women in the cabin locked in each other's arms, crying and exhibiting the most intense signs of terror and distress. They were all engulphed. The lamentations of the French and Germans were most painful, as I could easily distinguish their cries and shouts. . . .
>
> Besides the heart rending sight of so many woe-expressing faces, and hands uplifted in wild despair, or in agonizing appeal to heaven, and the awful cry which smote our ears in the last moment, one other incident sent a thrill of dread through our hearts. Just as the water was closing over the smoke-pipe, there rose up from the sea a sound like a heavy groan, or ocean sigh; caused, doubtless, by the steam and heat in the boiler, but it was a sound never to be forgotten.

A vortex formed where the liner had been just moments before. The swells flattened out and appeared to break around the oblong slick that calmed the sea. Vast bubbles rose to the surface and burst in rapid succession. The water boiled and tumbled. Amid the eddies and whirls, far below the slick, people felt themselves being drawn deeper and deeper into the water, and they were helpless to stop it from happening. The light faded. Their lungs ached for air. Many gave up, let the last breaths they would ever take disappear before their eyes as bubbles in the darkness, and sank down to join the ship. She was crashing into the sea floor and digging a trench in the soft sand before coming to rest, the air still escaping from pockets trapped inside the staterooms and saloons, as if she too were drowning.

Captain Luce struggled for life. He refused to give up. It was not in his nature:

> I was carried down a great distance, with my son Willie in my arms. I opened my eyes to see if I could discover light through the water. It was some time before I could do so, and then it seemed a very long time before I reached the surface. When I did so, I could only have held out a few moments. I saw Willie near me, with a life preserver on him, and after a brief struggling with my own helpless child in my arms . . . again I felt myself impelled downwards to a great depth, and before I reached the surface a second time had nearly perished, and lost the hold of my child.
>
> As I again struggled to the surface of the water, a most awful and heart-rending scene presented itself to my view—over two hundred men, women and children struggling together amidst pieces of wreck of every kind, calling on each other for help, and imploring God to assist them.

The living and the dead tossed together on the swells that rolled in to obliterate the slick and transform the surface of the ocean once more to its orderly procession of waves. Luce caught sight of Willie and swam toward him. From below, a dark form suddenly materialized. It grew larger as Luce swam fast toward his son, then flew out from the water to a great height. Luce immediately realized it was the paddle-wheel box he had been standing on moments earlier. Air trapped in the half-moon-shaped box, now splintered and fragmented, must have torn it loose from the inert hull hundreds of feet below. Its great momentum still strong, the paddle-wheel box crashed down on top of Willie's head, crushing his skull, and came sliding on toward Luce, grazing his head on its way by:

I struggled to get away, and on looking around I saw that the box was [still] sliding upon the water. A short distance back poor little Willie was lying dead. During my struggle I had cut my head badly, which caused it to bleed very profusely, and I was compelled for some time afterwards to wash it frequently, to keep the blood from blinding me.

The paddle-wheel box came to rest a short distance away from Luce. It floated upside down, its curve projecting below the water like the hull of a little boat. Enough of the frame remained intact to form low bulwarks. Luce swam to it and hauled himself aboard, landing face first in the water. He vomited up the sea that had found its way into his lungs. He tasted blood in his mouth, and he could hardly see. He warmed his numbed fingers in the wound as he ran his hand across his head to clear his sight. He rose to his knees, the water swirling around him. The box rolled and pitched in the swells, threatening to hurl him overboard.

Struggling to maintain his balance inside the confines of the box, which was about twelve square feet in size, Luce saw a rope attached to what was left of the door built into the box to allow the crew to gain access to the wheel to make repairs. He pulled the line across to each side of the frame and lashed it tight. With the rope spanning the width of the box, he found he could ride the swells without falling as long as he did not let go. He dragged himself to his feet to get himself out of the water, knowing it would soon steal away what strength remained in his bruised and battered body. Even standing up, it washed back and forth in the box well over the height of his knees. He shook from the cold and grief that gripped him. Blood rushed down his face and covered his clothes. Still, he did not give up.

Luce called to others around him to get in the box. George Allen thrashed on the surface of the ocean nearby. He heard his friend's voice, saw him standing in the box, and swam halfheartedly to it. His wife, Grace, and their infant son, Herbert, were both dead. He was convinced of it. Herbert had been in his arms as the ship went down, and the force of the water tore him free. Grace's screams echoed in his mind. He kept seeing the awful moment again and again, as he struggled in the water and finally clambered aboard the box with the captain. William Brown, his wife, and their child must surely have died too, as had Millie. The violence of the downward plunge into the sea was great. It had killed many of those aboard.

"Grab hold of my waist, George!" Luce said, as he hauled his companion into the box and helped him stand up. "I can keep my balance with the rope I've rigged."

Allen circled Luce with his arms and embraced him as a husband might a wife, sneaking up behind her in the kitchen to give her a hug while she prepared supper. Allen looked over Luce's shoulder at the horror still unfolding all around them and tried to close his eyes to block the scene from his sight. The sounds were terrible enough. But every time he did so, he lost his balance and almost dragged him and the captain overboard. He was forced to watch the men, women, and children dying. Their screams burned an impression deep in his mind, one that if he survived he never would quite shake loose or bury as the years passed. As he later confided to his immediate family, speaking of the disaster only once with the promise that it never be mentioned again, he believed others, including Captain Luce, whose own son was dead, felt the same way.

Another man made it to the box, the young German sailor Ferdinand Keyn. He clambered in and took his position behind Allen. Samuel Woodruff, the brother of Mary Ann Collins, also made it to the box. A Frenchman, an Englishman, and three other New Yorkers from the first-class cabin swam to them, and before getting in themselves they helped aboard Mrs. Wilkinson and her two children, whom Keyn recognized. Robert Wilkinson was *Arctic*'s second steward, a man known to many aboard the ship. With twelve people aboard, the box settled well down in the water. Finding it too crowded, one man jumped back into the sea to find what he considered a better spot on the top of a door.

As each castaway climbed in the box, one after the other, each individual in turn gripped the person in front around the waist to keep the box in proper trim and to avoid capsizing. A line of forlorn, bedraggled people formed, each holding on to the other as if they were engaged in a strange kind of dance formation. As the box rode up over a swell, they swayed and rocked together. It made for an odd and pitiful sight.

A lady passenger, Mrs. Cahill, floated in the water near the box, along with her female servant, both wearing life preservers. Her husband, an older man, did not have one on, and he began to drown in front of her. The paddle box drifted near him. Mrs. Cahill saw Luce trying to rescue others in the water.

"Captain!" she cried, "Captain, can you save my poor husband!"

Luce turned toward the direction of Mrs. Cahill's voice and observed her husband about to go down for the last time. With a mighty heave, he yanked him up over the side of the box. Mr. Cahill climbed in and began calling for his wife. The grief at seeing her rapidly drifting away to a certain fate overwhelmed him. A swell washed over the box, deluging all of them, and threw him out again.

"Captain!" Mrs. Cahill screamed.

Luce tried to reach the woman's husband. But he could not. Mr. Cahill drowned in front of them all. Again and again the same scene played itself out in merciless horror. Men and women fought over doors, and the victors of the combat, thinking themselves safe, were just as quickly catapulted back into the water. Others sought refuge on the water casks that had been lashed together and jettisoned to serve as tiny rafts. More frequently than not, the lashings worked loose and separated, relegating the passengers clinging to them to the sea. Some got caught between the casks as they parted and came together in the swells, and for them the fight for life ended swiftly in a blinding flash of intense pain, and the rapid filling of their lungs as they sank below the surface.

The large raft was its own stage of horror, a platform of loose spars and planks about forty feet in length and no more than four feet wide. Men, women, and children tried to climb on board over the bodies of those already embarked, pushing it down deep in the water from the heavy load. The waves swept them away, and yet they repeatedly tried to get back on. Many of the victims, mostly men, clung to the raft with only one hand.

Among the men on the raft was a waiter by the name of Peter McCabe, a young man from Dublin whom Luce had hired as one of the extra hands to tend the full roster of passengers booked in first class. This was his first ocean voyage. He considered himself lucky to have reached the raft and cursed at having been aboard the liner in the first place. Right after *Arctic* sank and he floated back up to the surface of the water, he had climbed up on a door. The door threatened to spill him into the sea with each passing swell, which encouraged him to leave it for others struggling to get on and swim over to a barrel. This was no better. He made his way to the raft, thinking it might provide a safer haven even if it was too crowded. He had seen what happened to others who preferred their own private places on the swells, riding the unstable doors, casks, boards, settees, and grates. Although he was not an experienced seaman, McCabe had a powerful amount of common sense.

Luce glanced toward the raft and shouted over his shoulder to Allen. "Look!"

When Allen saw his wife, Grace, he almost broke down with joy. She was not dead after all. She was hanging on to the raft with Millie, Clara Brown, Clara's female servant who served as the nurse to their now dead daughter, and William Brown. He called out to them, but they did not hear him. As they struggled among the mass of human beings piled on the raft, all they could know was that they were still alive, that they might yet live to see another day if a ship chanced by to rescue them before it was too late.

The wind drove the wreckage before it over the waves farther and farther out to sea. The debris and corpses and those still fighting to stay afloat began to separate. The darkness of the approaching night brought a curtain down to the east that crept closer as the minutes passed. The fog, still thick and heavy, came in and out, making it hard to keep track of the people floating on the wreckage. The large raft, heavy with its human cargo, drifted much more slowly to leeward than the lighter pieces of the steamer. Luce and the ten others with him in the box skittered across the tops of the swells to leeward at a quick rate. Soon their world became more solitary. The cries of the dying grew fainter.

The thirty-one men in Dorian's boat paddled hard to keep clear of the pockets of struggling people to avoid being swamped. They passed many "dead females" and the broken body of the "colored stewardess" Anna Downer. They noted in shock that the life preservers had in some cases hastened the deaths of the wearers, making their last minutes even more horrific.

When the liner sank, the force of the vortex pulled many of the crew and passengers down headfirst. The tumult ripped the life preservers from some of the men, allowing them to reach the surface with their heads above water. But the women ended up with the life preservers bunched at their hips, caught on their full skirts. As these unfortunate ladies floated back to the surface, they found themselves hanging by the lower portions of their bodies, heads and shoulders and upper torsos held down below the waves by the life preservers, their feet flailing above the surface in a futile attempt to pull themselves upright. It was an appalling spectacle, one the men in the boat did not forget.

Among the hardest of the men crammed in Dorian's boat was Patrick Tobbin. He observed the sights around him without compassion or evident emotion. He was just glad he was not one of the people he saw in the water, that he had at last found a place of relative security in a lifeboat. Overloaded as it was and with only six inches of the rails showing above the cold ocean, he still counted himself as one of the luckiest members of the liner's company. "After the Arctic disappeared we saw a large number floating about, still alive, but we could save none. Our little boat was filled to its utmost capacity. So we had to leave them to perish from the cold—the water is always cold on the Banks—and as prey to the fishes."

Drawn by the commotion and the blood in the water, the sharks came in great numbers. There was at least some mercy in the end for many of the passengers. They drowned or died from hypothermia before the sharks ate them alive. The handful of survivors, those on the large raft and the smaller ones with two or three embarked, in the paddle box with Luce, and aboard Dorian's boat numbered just over one hundred. Before the night was through, nearly all of them would be dead. But for the moment, the struggle for life went on as the wind and tide scattered the wreckage across an ever widening swath of water—cold, desolate, and becoming more tempestuous by the hour as the gale that had been building increased in strength and moved slowly toward them.

CHAPTER SIXTEEN

BATTLE FOR LIFE

THE TWILIGHT SLOWLY DEEPENED, draping the sea in a cloak of darkness that obscured the limited horizon visible through the fog. The vast, rolling hills of water flecked with white crests became less distinct in the fading light. But their presence was made known to every sense of the people riding beam to the swells in the paddle-wheel box as it rose and fell. The larger swells began to break. The box rose up the precipitous faces of the swells. The crests broke over the people in the box and departed with a hiss of boiling cold foam. Increasing amounts of water sloshed inside the box. With no bailer, it rose higher and might soon swamp the craft. The temperature dropped, and the wind blew walls of damp fog to the east, adding to the misery of the castaways, all of whom expected to die.

The two children were the first to go, the last of those who had gone aboard the liner. Although their mother tried her best to keep them from falling, she could not stop the inevitable exhaustion from robbing them of their feeble strength. Weak from the cold, hunger, and the struggle to remain standing, they stayed brave to the last, until each in turn dropped down on the boards of the box and were immediately washed away when a larger-than-usual swell swept over them. They did not cry out. There was a thud, a splash, and then the mother's muffled sobs. That was all. Soon she too gave up, her will to live gone, having lost all that was dear to her. She teetered for a moment, losing her balance, and dropped down onto the boards where the sea could easily reach her. When another big swell broke against the frail craft, the deep claimed her as well, leaving only the men.

George Allen held fast to Luce, and as he fought to stay on his feet, the hope burned bright in his heart that his wife still lived, that somewhere out in the black void closing in around them she rode with the others on the raft. He did not know that they too had gone—that in fact every woman and child aboard *Arctic* was now dead, nearly one-third of all the souls who had set sail in her just a week before. Only the men remained, and one by one, they were dying.

Several miles away on the large raft, the heavy seas and the bone-chilling cold took their toll. Peter McCabe watched helplessly as the number of dead increased with every passing crest:

> There we were, in the midst of the ocean, without the slightest hope of assistance, while every minute one or more of our unfortunate fellow passengers were dropping into their watery grave from sheer exhaustion. Those who had life preservers did not sink, but floated with their ghastly faces upwards, reminding those who still remained alive of the fate that awaited them. . . . Some of them floated off, and were eaten and gnawed by fishes, while others were washed under the raft, and remained with me till I was rescued. I could see their faces in the openings as they were swayed to and fro by the waves, which threatened every moment to wash me off. . . .
>
> Very few words were spoken by any, and the only sound that we heard was the splash of the waters or the heavy breathing of the poor sufferers, as they tried to recover their breath after a wave had passed over them. Nearly all were submerged to their arm pits, while a few could with great difficulty keep their heads above the surface. The women were the first to go. They were unable to stand the exposure more than three or four hours. They all fell off the raft without a word, except one poor girl, who cried out, in intense agony, "Oh, my poor mother and sisters."

Not far from Luce and the rest in the paddle box, four other small rafts drifted in company. These along with bits of debris were caught in the same branch of the Labrador Current, which, together with the tide and the influence of the wind, shepherded the wreckage on its way out to sea while drawing it farther from the raft and Dorian's lifeboat. The banks were filled with currents that merged and diverged like unseen rivers. The men on the rafts went in one direction, McCabe and Dorian in another. Although Luce had seen no others alive on wreckage before the light faded altogether, he, like others adrift nearby, suspected there might be additional survivors, and indeed there were.

Jassonet François rode his tiny boards with the messboy, a young man of about twenty. The old Frenchman had seen much during his long life at sea. He had endured storms, hunger, cold, and fatigue. He had fought hard in barroom brawls. Although he was frightened, cold, and hungry like the rest, he knew more than most of the others how busy the waters of the Grand Banks were in late September, with so many vessels putting out to sea bound for home ports in France. He clung to his hope that the fog might lift and a ship might sail close enough to spot him. In the meantime, he resolved to hold on. Daybreak held the promise of life, and he intended to stay alive long enough to see it come.

The boy with him, though, did not have the years of experience at sea to fall back on. He shivered and cried out in pain from the hunger and thirst that afflicted him. He had some biscuits with him, but he had difficulty eating them because his tongue was swollen. He could hardly swallow. What he wanted most was water. Jassonet cradled him in his arms to try to warm him and find some relief himself from the cold. The young man's head rested on Jassonet's broad shoulders. He talked to him, gave him words of comfort, though he knew the messboy could not understand a word of French. He called him his *compagnon de voyage*.

Five of *Arctic*'s firemen, some of them villains, others loyal members of the crew who had helped Dorian build the raft, floated over the swells on two separate rafts, one with two and the other with three of the men aboard. Their pieces of wreckage were so small none of them could sit down without capsizing the planks and ending their struggle. They stood back-to-back, propped up like unsteady towers. As each swell came and went, they had to bend their knees and sway opposite the roll to avoid being flipped over. Their muscles stiffened from the cold and pain.

The luckiest man in the area was James Smith. A religious man, he prayed to God for help, and in his case, it appeared that God listened. Just before the night eclipsed all the ambient light, for there were no stars or moon to show through the fog, Smith made two amazing discoveries:

I discovered close by me a large square basket lined with tin, floating lightly by me—one of the stewards' dish baskets it proved to be—and, paddling up to it, I got it on board, and with the help of a small piece of rope I had round my shoulders, I lashed it pretty firmly on top of the plank, thus not only tending to make my raft more secure, but affording me a comparatively dry place to sit on the edge of it, and with my feet inside, forming a shelter for my legs up as high as my knees.

After getting all this arranged, and while sitting and watching the water as to the weight on the raft [the waves were filling the basket], I was again surprised to hear a distinct rattle against the side of the raft, which proving to be a small airtight tin can, a part of a set of such used as a life-preserver—I seized hold of it as an additional token of the presence of a protecting Providence. I cut out one end of it with my pocket knife, and found it answered the purpose of what above anything else I then needed—a baling pot—and by which I was enabled to keep my little shelter clear of water, and so acceptable as a protection from the cold, damp blast, did I find this little willow house, that I soon found myself cramped down into the inside, thus keeping not only my feet and legs but the lower part of my body something warm.

The nighttime minutes seemed to last for hours, the hours an eternity. The survivors summoned all of the reserves of strength they could muster to cling to the life that appeared so near to falling away. The waves swept past, often breaking over them. The Englishman with Luce's party relaxed his hold on the man in front of him and slipped over the side. Now there were only seven men left on the paddle-wheel box.

As the night passed, Luce stared ahead into the complete darkness, lost in the thoughts that plagued him. He saw the very same paddle box that had saved him rush from the sea like some strange monster and kill his boy. Again and again, the box roared up from the depths. His place of duty for so many years, the fact that it now served as the only barrier between him and the deep was cruel and ironic. At what cost had he been spared? It was almost too much to contemplate. He relived moments he could not banish from his mind.

His strength ebbing, he thought of Elizabeth. Willie's death would strike her deep. And he thought of Robert. Robert would be in college, up in Troy. He had started school on this very day, the day all of their lives were changed forever by a disaster at sea. If Luce did not live, what would become of them both? He willed himself to stay strong for them, his only remaining family. He must not die. He must fight on and return to them if he could.

Luce became aware of a wind shift. Based on the feel of the wind on his cheeks, he could tell its relative direction in relation to the swells. The fresh breeze had earlier blown from a west-southwesterly quarter. It had now backed to the southeast, coming in just as cold and raw as ever, but a bad sign. The gale he had thought might hover near appeared to have moved closer. If his experience proved right, and he believed it would, the wind would keep backing until it came in strong from the northeast as the low-pressure system swooped down on them.

Time, it seemed, was running short, the sand almost gone from the hourglass:

> At last the wished for morning came, surrounded with a dense fog—not a living soul to be seen but our own party—seven men being left. In the course of the morning we saw some water casks and other things belonging to our ship, but nothing that we could get to afford us any relief.
>
> Our raft was rapidly settling, as it absorbed water.
>
> About noon Mr. S. M. Woodruff, of New York [Mrs. Collins's brother], was relieved by death. All the others now began to suffer very severely for want of water, except Mr. George Allen and myself. In this respect we were very much favored, although we had not a drop on the raft. The day continued foggy, except just at noon, as near as we could judge, we had a clear horizon for about half an hour, and nothing could be seen but water and sky.

James Smith passed the morning of September 28 in a similarly somber mood. He too noted the brief lifting of the fog:

> About mid-day the sun cleared away the mist, and the heat of his rays was truly grateful, but Oh how desolate in its very cheerfulness seemed the prospect he thus unfolded. Over the whole broad expanse of waters, not a sail could be seen—nothing save the figures of the two firemen about a half a mile distant, still standing erect, and showing themselves at intervals, as every heavy swell would raise them on its crest. I had not yet felt either hunger or thirst, for which I was truly thankful, for I had but a handful of dry, broken crackers [stashed away] in my hat, which I felt determined to save to the last, and of course no water. I dreaded the cravings of either.

By noon on September 28, Jassonet François found himself at sea with a corpse:

> [The] young man died on the morning of the 28th, from the effects of cold and hunger. The cold had taken such a hold of him that it became impossible for him to utter a single word. I took him in my arms and supported his head on my shoulder. When he breathed his last sigh, he gave me such a violent shock that he was near upsetting me into the sea. I attached him to the raft with cords, and I kept him for about twenty hours, at the expiration of which, finding that he was really dead, and apprehending the visit of some large sharks, I [threw him into the sea].

More hours passed. The men with Luce and Allen grew weaker, and some of them became delirious from want of food and water and the lack of sleep. Just before *Arctic* sank, Allen had rushed back into the dining saloon and grabbed food from the table. He had given some to Grace, Millie, and William and Clara and then had run back and found still more food, but by this time the ship was starting to settle low in the water. The roar below in the hull from the inrushing flood thundered. He saw a boiled chicken on a platter, jammed the fowl into his coat pocket, and raced back to his wife's side, taking Herbert from her at her request, promising to keep him safe. Now, with the men in the box in severe pain from hunger and thirst, he brought out his boiled chicken and divided much of it with the rest of those aboard. He kept a little back, though, thinking they might need it later.

Ravenous, Ferdinand Keyn wolfed down the bits of chicken. It served only to whet his appetite. He reached into his pocket for the biscuits he had taken from the dining saloon. They were a mass of dough soaked in brine. He ate them anyway, over the objections and warnings of his companions. The thirst assailing him in previous hours increased as the day wore on. Keyn became feverish, weak, and delirious. He begged for water, but no one aboard the box had any to give.

"Water, I must have water," Keyn muttered. As the hours passed, the more crazed he became. The moment of insanity came suddenly even so. With both hands supporting him on either side of the box, Keyn stooped and lapped up the sea like a horse at the edge of a river.

"No!" Luce shouted. "You'll poison yourself!"

Allen reached back and pulled Keyn to his feet. "Easy, boy. You'll just make it worse."

Keyn said nothing. However, his face was wild with pain and fear. He did not know how much longer he could stand his ordeal. His tongue swelled up from the salt. His stomach burned. His muscles ached beyond anything he ever had experienced. Suddenly, he gave a hoarse shout and leaped over the side of the paddle box. He dove deep and was about to breathe in the sea, but as he burst to the surface, the five other men still in the box seized hold of him and dragged him back aboard.

The day progressed in this way, each man struggling in his own private battle to stay alive. Not much was said between them, just the occasional word or two of encouragement, an urging for them all to hang on until they sighted a ship. But as the afternoon light began to wane, their hopes flickered and almost left them. Soon it was 4:45 P.M., a full day since *Arctic* sank. The box settled deeper into the waves, its wood heavy from the water it had absorbed. The darkness approached, and they realized no ship would see them. Now they were sure they would die. How could they live through yet another night? Fog enveloped them in its cold, damp embrace. Three more men fell to the boards and were washed away, leaving only Luce, Allen, and Keyn. Their minds dulled from exhaustion, they watched the bodies of their companions float atop the swells and disappear quickly in the mist. Not a word was spoken. There was nothing to say.

The three men took turns sitting down on a trunk that had drifted near enough for them to snag and haul aboard the paddle box, affording them a chance to rest their legs and buy them more time until the box sank, the gale came, or they died of the cold and hunger. Inside the trunk, they discovered the belongings of one of the nurses who had sailed with them to care for one of the passengers' infants. Seeing these items meant for the care of babies, oddly out of place on the heaving, lonely sea, reminded them all of the bitter loss so many had suffered and would suffer once the news of the liner's sinking reached New York. Of the three men, the nurse's trunk proved the saddest reminder for Allen. September 28 would have been little Herbert's first birthday. They tied a white garment around the tip of a long, slender pole ripped from the box's frame to use as a signal, if a ship ever did appear.

Luce was the last person to sit down on the trunk. Exhausted after twenty-seven hours on his feet, he fell into a fitful sleep. Like the rest, he had eaten a small morsel of the boiled chicken. The simple pleasure of eating and sleeping was sweet, and it gave Luce strength to hang on for a little while longer. He suddenly jolted awake and heard voices calling him. Peering into the darkness, he thought he saw a naked child flitting above the waves. It looked bright, like an angel, seeming to glow as it flew. Luce rubbed his eyes, squeezed them closed, opened his eyes again, and still saw the child. He realized then that he was seeing things, hallucinations brought on from his ordeal, the pain, and fatigue. The child hovered near, then disappeared into the night.

CHAPTER SEVENTEEN

RESCUE

THE FIRST HINT of the coming dawn on Friday, September 29, appeared to the east as a slight diminishing of the depth of the coal black void that surrounded the men in the paddle-wheel box. The darkness was still impenetrable, the fog still thick. Yet as the sun inched over the invisible horizon, the tops of the waves created a demarcation of light and dark, the ocean in shadow, the sky evolving into a faint gray. The men swayed back and forth and from side to side, struggling to keep their balance on the rising crests. The wind had shifted to the northeast, just as Luce expected, and he knew their end must certainly come soon. The wind and swells now corresponded, coming at them from about the same direction. The ocean had assumed its state of harmony, a sure sign of what lay ahead in a matter of only hours.

Luce kept hold of the rope rigged across the width of the box, but every minute proved an agony. The line chafed away the skin on the inside of his fingers and his palms, and cut into his raw flesh. The saltwater on the line burned. He tasted the salt from the flying spray every time his dry tongue ran across his blistered and cracked lips. It caked his face and mustache and stung the gash in his head through the soft clots of blood that had formed on it. He continued to hallucinate, and in his quasi-derangement, he entertained the prospect of death. He had fought hard, tried his best, and that was all any man could do.

Out of the swirling fog a light suddenly materialized. At first Luce thought it was another false image, an apparition conjured from his delirium. But it grew larger and seemed quite close.

"George," Luce whispered. "George. A light!"

Allen and Keyn looked eastward, and both of them saw the white orb of a ship's light glowing with a halo around it from the fog. Screaming as loudly as they could manage, they cried for help. They could not see the ship. It was still too dark and the atmosphere was too filled with vapor to make out her form. For fifteen minutes, the men yelled for help and prayed to God that their calls might reach the lookout posted at the bow of the passing vessel. Slowly and steadily, though, she moved on out of sight, leaving the men feeling more hopeless and exhausted than ever.

With a groan, Keyn let go of Allen and sat down on the trunk. In the dim light of dawn, Luce and Allen looked on in horror as Keyn slowly and deliberately withdrew a pen knife from his shirt pocket and opened the blade. He stared at his left wrist, an insane look in his eye. Without saying a word, he plunged the tip of his knife into his wrist.

"Stop!" Luce shouted, though his voice sounded far away to him, as if someone else had called to the young man.

A spurt of blood erupted from the puncture and ran down Keyn's hand. Keyn brought the wound to his lips and sucked greedily. He let the blood pump into his mouth and flow down his throat to his empty stomach. It smeared all over his face before Allen reached him, and with a deep sigh of despair and empathy, grabbed hold of Keyn's arms and yanked him to his feet. "Do you want to die? Do you?"

"Yes," Keyn muttered. "I want death to come."

Allen shook his head and tore off a piece of his shirt, wrapping it tightly around the young man's wrist to stop the bleeding. The wound was not deep. It would not kill him as long as the bandage remained tightly bound.

"Give the captain your knife," Allen said.

Dazed, Keyn just stared at the waves, now clearly visible in the increasing light. They were the big, true seas that marked the start of the gale. The wind began to come in fresh, and it contained the hard, cold bite of winter. Allen snatched the knife away from Keyn and gave it to

Luce. Both he and Luce told him to keep fighting. They had lost too many people to death already, they said. They must have faith in what the new day might bring. Keyn settled down a little, but he continued to mutter incomprehensibly in German.

The sun gradually lit up the sea around the men in the familiar dull gray world. The colorless hues of the sea and sky presented a scene of utter and complete desolation. The fog lifted a little, and the curtains of gray parted.

And then the sail of a ship apparently headed in their direction hove into view. Luce waved the signal they had made from the strip of wood and the garment found in the trunk. When he grew too tired to go on, he passed the signal to Allen. Keyn's spirits seemed to have recovered at the sight of the ship. He helped wave the signal as well.

The ship sailed toward them. But not close enough. As the time progressed, it became clear to the men that she would also sail away without discovering them. This second disappointment nearly broke Keyn. He again threw himself into the sea, and it was with great difficulty that Luce and Allen, both summoning strength they had long thought gone, hauled him back aboard the box. He sat on the trunk and wept.

Not far away, though out of view of the men in the paddle box, James Smith occupied himself in keeping warm by paddling toward the two firemen still adrift near his "little willow house":

The morning dawned again, and with it a horrid scene of despair at the gloomy prospect of the same dense foggy atmosphere now and then fully developing to view the same two erect figures [the firemen nearest to Smith] dancing about on the rolling surf, and in my selfish liberality I bargained with myself that I would endure still during this day, seeing that my two companions were obliged to be on their feet supporting each other in a very precarious looking back-to-back attitude, were able still to exist. I felt a little hungry this morning and ate half a biscuit.

While warming myself by about two hours paddling up towards them, during which the fog partially cleared away, and while close to them, we all became excited at the sight of a sail. . . . I had little hope of [the ship] coming much nearer, but being determined to leave no effort untried which might possibly attract their notice, I stripped myself and taking off my shirt tied it by the sleeves to the end of my paddle, and with my handkerchief on a small strip of wood tied on above it, I thought I had a tolerably conspicuous signal, and waved it to and fro for more than an hour, until the ship was nearly out of sight—and just as I had lowered it, in utter hopelessness, we all descried at the same instant, in the opposite direction, another sail—end on us—just entering as it were into our grand amphitheatre through a cloud of mist that seemed to rise and clear away above the vessel, forming a grand triumphal archway around our eureka like a tower of promise in the centre.

Feeling sure, at first sight, that this one was standing towards us, I did not remain long undeceived, for she began to increase in size as time slowly wore on, and although she was falling to leeward considerably as she advanced, still I felt sure if she kept on the same tack she would undoubtedly see our signals before passing beyond.

The fog lifted away in the vicinity of the paddle-wheel box as well, and this time it was George Allen who spied the third ship sighted that day. He shouted to Luce and Keyn. Both of them followed his gaze, their hope surfacing yet one more time. Luce observed the same arch in the fog that Smith was seeing that very moment:

About fifteen minutes after Keyn was rescued from self-destruction a second time, Mr. Allen discovered a sail standing for us. She was about seven miles off. She was seen through an arch which seemed to form in the fog, and gave us a clear view through it directly in the line of the ship. She continued standing toward us, but after a while changed her course. Upon this our spirits again drooped.

Jassonet François observed the ship the others had seen. He also tried to signal her:

After being at the mercy of the waves for a couple of days and nights—that is to say, fifty-two hours—on the 29th, towards ten in the morning, I perceived to the west a sail which seemed to be approaching me; then, with the small plank which had served me as an oar, I was enabled to make some signals, which did not seem to be noticed by the vessel. I continued to [drift] for another hour, and I then became convinced that the vessel was coming directly towards me. This gave me a little courage, for my strength had begun to abandon me. I made a fresh signal, and I saw that they perceived me, for the vessel came straight towards me.

All was in a state of orderly chaos aboard the full-rigged ship *Cambria*. The lookout's call that there was a man in the water brought Captain John Russell to the rail with his spyglass. He lifted the glass, squinted through the lens, and spied a lone man standing on a tiny raft made of planks, waving a board to and fro. The man looked old and bedraggled, the perfect image of a castaway. *Cambria* closed rapidly with the man on the raft, so quickly in fact that Russell knew he would not have time to heave his ship to before he might possibly lose sight of him in the fog that had been rolling in and out that morning.

"Get some lines trailed astern," he ordered his first officer. "Send Mister Ross into the fore chains with a line. He'll have to go in and get the poor fellow."

The first officer carried out the master's orders. Crewmen uncoiled ropes and threw them overboard for the man in the water to catch if Ross, the second mate, lost hold of him. Ross hurried forward. He climbed up over the bulwarks with a line neatly coiled to allow it to run free and tied the end of it to the shrouds. The ship came up on top of a wave, high above the man on the raft.

It was now or never. The second mate dove over the side of the ship, almost losing his breath in the cold water, and swam to the man on the raft. He grabbed him as *Cambria* sailed on by and tied the rope around the man's waist. As the line pulled taut, the forward motion of the vessel towed them both under. They fought for air and burst to the surface. Several strong crewmen heaved on the line. In a few moments, both men came over the bulwarks. Jassonet François clutched the shrouds for support, but he did not fall. Captain Russell approached him and asked what had happened. As a reply, the captain received a flurry of rapidly spoken French mixed with broken English. Something about a shipwreck, other survivors.

Jassonet pointed and jabbed the air to windward. He swung his arm to show the direction in which the others might be found. He made signs with his hands, pretending they were rafts rolling on the waves. Captain Russell ordered his officers to take the Frenchman below to the forecastle, to get him dry clothes and some food and water. He climbed to the main top and scanned the ocean. To his amazement, he discovered four other pieces of wreckage carrying human freight scattered over several square miles. Praying that the fog did not close in thick again, Russell put *Cambria* about and headed for the nearest raft, with three men on it. After he picked them up, he was prepared to beat back to the others he had seen, tiny and indistinct in the haze, but real enough just the same, and at the total mercy of the rising gale. He raised his glass again. What on earth were the three men he saw standing in? he wondered.

It took time, but the ship finally reached the first group of victims. Captain Russell ordered the main topsail backed, and *Cambria* came to rest, plunging and rolling in the seas. His men lowered a boat, unshipped the oars, and worked with a will. Every stroke brought them closer to the men. When they came alongside, the crew noted with surprise that the three castaways were standing in an overturned fragment of a paddle box. They hauled them into the boat, where they promptly collapsed, one of them saying he was the captain of the mail steamer *Arctic* and that there likely were others adrift in the immediate area.

From his vantage point, Smith and the two firemen near him became alarmed. They had no idea if they had been seen, but they knew the ship had discovered something—in all likelihood, another band of survivors. Perhaps the vessel stopped for the three other firemen Smith had seen on a raft before he lost sight of them the previous evening:

When within about two or three miles of us, and about an hour and a half after she first hove in sight, we were relieved by her backing her sails, altering her course, and laying to for a while, then hoisting a signal up her spanker gaff, she put about and bore away, on and on far in the distance on the opposite tack until my heart began to fail again doubting whether she was beating to windward for us, or had gone on her way rejoicing in the discovery and rescue of only a portion of the unfortunate wretches within range of her.

But again, how light and buoyant was the joy as she at last put about, and standing directly for us; on and on she advanced like a saving angel, until we could see her noble looking hull distinctly rise and fall within little over a mile distant from us, when she backed her sails again, and waited for some time. . . .

Soon she filled away again, and at last, laying to close by the two firemen. I saw her boat lowered with five men in it, who picking up the two firemen in their course, came dashing along direct for my raft, and soon banging alongside, I allowed myself to tumble aboard of them, unable physically to adopt any thing of a graceful action, and morally overpowered with gratitude to God and to these his instruments. I remained speechless until I got on board the ship.

With the last of the survivors safely aboard *Cambria*—Jassonet François, Captain Luce, George Allen, Ferdinand Keyn, James Smith, and the five firemen—Captain Russell put his ship about once more and doubled back over the area in search of others. He searched until dusk settled over the ocean and made additional efforts useless in the deteriorating weather and darkness. Reluctantly, he set his course for Cabot Strait and the Gulf of St. Lawrence beyond.

Later that night, as *Cambria* ran under shortened sail before the northeasterly gale, the wind howling in the rigging and the waves breaking astern in towering crests, Captain Luce lay in his bunk under a pile of wool blankets, his head bandaged in a length of white linen. He listened to the storm, the stamp of feet on the deck above him. Although he was warm and safe, he felt a deep sense of misery. He thought of Willie, and of Elizabeth and Robert, who would think he and Willie were both dead. He thought of the dire circumstances of any others who might still be out there on bits of the wreck, alone on a now-angry sea. What of the raft Dorian had built? The lifeboats? What of them? Despite his exhaustion, his tortured thoughts robbed him of sleep. At last, though, his body's need for rest overcame him, and he lost consciousness.

CHAPTER EIGHTEEN

DISTRESSING
NEWS

THE PILOT BOAT *Christian Berg* sailed slowly among the ships lying to their anchors west of Governors Island, their forms almost invisible in the darkness save for the yellow flicker of the riding lamps that warned the helmsman to steer clear. Off the bow, the low skyline of Manhattan cut a swath in the night speckled with the occasional glow from a window. Most of the city's half-million residents rested in their beds, the workday ahead still many hours away. However, not all of the city's inhabitants slept. The brothels and taverns teemed with men on this late Tuesday night of October 10. Lights burned in the bakeries and along the docks, where the fishermen brought their catches for sale in the markets. The editorial offices and press rooms of the major daily newspapers were lit up as well. Reporters finished writing their stories while other employees set the type and inked the presses for Wednesday's early morning editions.

The crew of *Christian Berg* worked the schooner in close to the Battery and brought her smoothly alongside a pier on the East River. The sails fluttered in the light breeze, sheets eased to run free and rob the canvas of its power to drive the vessel. In a short time, the fore and main sails were brailed in, the jib dropped and secured at the bow. Lingering on the dock, a reporter from the *New York Herald* watched as the pilot boat was snugged down. The red nub at the tip of his cigar brightened each time he drew the smoke into his mouth. The pilots serving New York were the first to learn of any important news that came in with the inbound ships they guided across the shoals of Sandy Hook bar, and it was customary for the newspapers to keep a man on the piers to pick up word from the pilots of any breaking stories. The reporter yawned, stretched, pulled his coat tight against the cold of the late evening air, and walked quickly to the gangway of the schooner to find out if she had a scoop for him.

The dark forms of men appeared at the bulwarks, talking in low voices. The reporter noted that there were far more than the usual number of men aboard the schooner, and he became quite interested, his instincts stirred, as he watched them leave the boat. They looked ragged and tired. Some of them limped. Others were bandaged, and one man had his arm in a sling. The reporter stopped some of the men and asked who they were.

He could scarcely believe what he heard. Wrecked? More than three hundred dead? Steamship *Arctic?*

The story tumbled from the men who wished to talk, while others went on their way to find a room for the night or the comfort of a strong drink at one of the waterfront bars. One man in particular, George Burns, an expressman from Adams & Co., seemed to relish the attention. He said he had been a passenger aboard *Arctic*, which went down on September 27 after a collision with another steamship. He and thirty-one other survivors, including the ship's third officer, Francis Dorian, were picked up the following day by a Canadian bark, the *Huron*, bound for Quebec. The day after that, she met up with the ship *Lebanon* bound for New York, and eighteen of the survivors transferred to her, while the rest, all of them crewmen, for reasons of their own, refused to take passage back to Manhattan and decided to go to Canada. They had just arrived at the quarantine station on Staten Island a couple of hours earlier and were taken up to the city aboard *Christian Berg.*

The reporter listened carefully, writing down everything Burns said. This, he thought, was going to blow the top off the metropolis.

Arctic was the pride of the city, and many of her passengers moved in the highest circles of the elite and wealthy members of the upper classes. The fact that the wife and two children of Edward Knight Collins were lost and presumed dead added spice to an already incredible tale. The reporter rushed off to the offices of the *Herald* and filed his copy. The next morning, the following headlines and lead paragraph ran on the front page of the *Herald,* along with a full statement from George Burns:

DISTRESSING NEWS
Terrible Collision between Two Ocean Steamships and
TOTAL LOSS OF THE ARCTIC
Between Three and Four Hundred Souls Perished.
Only Thirty-two Lives Known to be Saved
Probable Loss of a British Steamship with a Regiment of Troops
on Board
LIST OF THE RESCUED
Names of the passengers on board the Arctic, &c.,&c.,&c.

At a late hour last evening we received the heart-rending intelligence of the loss of the Collins steamship Arctic. Captain Luce, the wife, daughter and son of E. K. Collins, Mr. Sandford, and many citizens of this city, besides more than three hundred of the passengers and crew have met a watery grave. The noble steamer, with her freight of stark corpses, is now surging to and fro beneath the surface of the billows of the Atlantic. Leaving more extended remarks upon the awful catastrophe for a future occasion, we hasten to introduce the account furnished us by Mr. George H. Burns, the express messenger of Adams & Co., who was on board, and fortunately escaped the terrible perils of the disaster.

As the news of the shipwreck swept through the city, flags were lowered to half-mast. Businesses closed. Crowds of people with loved ones and friends aboard *Arctic* descended on the offices of the Collins Line, hoping for some word, some shred of hope. In the Court of Common Trials, an attorney and good friend of Captain Luce opened the day's session with the following speech and a request to adjourn out of respect for the dead, which was granted:

> Some of my brethren of the bar requested me to suggest to your Honor that in view of the recent appalling calamity, the action consequent upon it in the other branch of this court, and in conformity with a custom long established and observed, this tribunal should transact no business today. I am sorry that some other gentleman did not undertake the melancholy duty of making this suggestion.
>
> The loss of the steamship Arctic—an affliction which touches not only this community, but the whole nation—comes upon me with a most painful effect. In that vessel, after a sojourn in Europe, during which I sometimes doubted whether I would ever again see my native land, I returned to my family and friends, the delights of home, and the profession of which I feel it is an honor to be a member. I formed the acquaintance of Captain Luce under circumstances which so endeared him to me that I can say without affectation, I loved him. If a noble ship could confer honor on the gallant sailor by whose command of her she was also dignified, there never was an instance in which such an association would be more likely to produce such a result. He was a most able officer, a sincere, right hearted man, and if he has indeed perished, it is consoling to know that he died at his post of duty, and in the chivalric discharge of his trust.
>
> It seems certain that the terrible disaster which engulphed his ship must have carried agony to hearts and homes in every district of our land, and perhaps some of the jurors present have had riven, by this dispensation, ties which bound their af-

fection to some beloved object. I tremble in apprehension for one who is reported, as among those who took to the boats, a highly valued friend, the companion of my early youth, to whom my devotion has strengthened with each succeeding hour of our lives.

But even those who are so fortunate as to have had no friend or acquaintance lost or endangered, cannot, if they feel an interest in our country's prosperity and character, fail, while deploring the dreadful sacrifice of so many lives, to mourn over the destruction of a vessel to which we might well feel a national pride. To the New York bar this awful incident is peculiarly distressing, as several of our brethren are known to have been in the Arctic, and there is scarcely a hope that they will ever again appear among us in the field of our professional association and labor. It seems, therefore, eminently proper that this Court should adjourn.

The shock of the tragedy struck deepest among those with loved ones aboard *Arctic*. James Brown collapsed in agony at the loss of his two daughters, eldest son, two grandchildren, daughter-in-law, and son-in-law. He did not yet know that George Allen had survived. Mrs. Brown fell into a catatonic-like state, unable to speak. She went into immediate seclusion far from the public eye and the assertive efforts of reporters to get quotes for their stories. Edward Knight Collins sought refuge from the public and the press at his home in Larchmont. The *New York Daily Times* described him as becoming a "maniac" in the extent of his grief, that he had suffered a nervous breakdown and was not expected to live. Up in Yonkers, the town mourned for their brave captain. Mrs. Elizabeth Fearing Luce dressed in black and kept to the house while she waited for Robert to come home from Troy.

There was one brief note of happiness in connection with Francis Dorian. He had remained aboard *Lebanon* as she lay to her anchor

Tuesday night off the quarantine station. Her master, Captain Story, had asked if he would stay aboard to help sail the vessel into port. Dorian was only too happy to honor the captain's request. He knew the public interest in the shipwreck would run high as soon as the survivors taken up to Manhattan aboard *Christian Berg* told their stories to the press. He wanted no part of that, though he inevitably was caught up in the story anyway. When *Lebanon* reached her berth on Wednesday afternoon, he gave a very brief statement and rushed to his wife and children on Hudson Street, where he embraced them with the deepest of emotions. He swept the tears from his wife's face. She called him a hero, said that was what the papers called him. No, he said. All he had done was his duty.

Reporters flocked to the Seamen's Retreat on Staten Island, where some of the injured and destitute sailors were taken for medical treatment. They interviewed Peter McCabe, the sole survivor on Dorian's raft out of seventy-two men and four women. They interviewed a handful of others as well, and they wrote long stories in vivid detail recounting the horrors experienced aboard *Arctic* and the raft—details that did much to increase the pain of those who had lost family and friends in the disaster. The reporter for the *New York Herald* jotted down the following description of McCabe's injuries as well as the "painfully interesting particulars of his escape from the wreck" for publication the next day:

> When we visited [Peter McCabe] yesterday at the Seamen's Retreat, on Staten Island, he did not appear like a man who required the care of a physician; and had we not seen the extent of his injuries before we left, we should have thought he had perfectly recovered from the effect of his long exposure. One of his feet, however, is in a horribly lacerated condition, large pieces of the flesh having been torn from it by rubbing against the raft, laying the bone in many places quite bare. The skin has also been torn from his fingers, and both of his hands have a parboiled appearance.

The editorial offices of all the newspapers hummed with activity on Wednesday, October 11, as the story broke and the city went into a state of shock and grief. The reporters gathering the information from the survivors began to realize that there was far more than a tragic occurrence, a mishap of the sea to write about. Statements from some of the survivors seemed to indicate that much of the crew had abandoned the ship long before she sank, that only Captain Luce and Third Officer Francis Dorian had remained with her to the last in heroic efforts to save as many passengers as possible. The writers and editors found this discovery disturbing, but they did not yet make much of the news. Information was still coming in, and it was too early to make rash judgments.

Apart from the immediate testimony of survivors brought in aboard the ship *Lebanon* and later transferred to *Christian Berg* the previous night, an encouraging dispatch arrived from Halifax: other survivors in two of *Arctic*'s boats had reached Newfoundland on September 29, after forty-two hours at sea. In these boats were twenty-eight crewmen, fourteen male passengers, and three of the ship's officers, though, unfortunately, not Captain Luce. This brought the total number of the rescued to seventy-seven. Not one survivor thus far, however, was a woman or child. Oddly, they were mostly crewmen, and this seemed to give credence to the stories starting to surface about the potentially sinister events that had taken place on the stricken steamship.

The dispatch was from Second Officer William Baalham, and it reported that a search for additional survivors and the ship's three missing boats produced negative results. Baalham provided his version of events, which were set in type ready for publication in the paper's Thursday morning edition, along with statements from McCabe and several others.

On Thursday morning, crowds of people gathered around the newsboys as soon as the papers hit the streets. They paid their two cents and hurried off to read more about the biggest tragedy to hit New York in recent memory:

New York Herald, Thursday, October 12
THE GREAT DISASTER
THE WRECK OF THE STEAMSHIP ARCTIC

In our regular edition, yesterday morning, we were obliged to record one of the greatest calamities that has ever befallen the city of New York; and, indeed, the loss of a noble steamship line the Arctic, unexcelled in the history of naval architecture, with so many valuable lives, must be considered a great national affliction.

But a few days ago the Arctic's passengers were rejoicing in the prospect of a speedy passage, and many a fair cheek was flushed with delight at the thought of the coming meeting with the dear ones at home. Even when the accident occurred, the extent of the danger was not known; and, finally, in one moment, more than three hundred men, women and children—in the full enjoyment of all that makes life dear to its possessor—was hurried to their death. No monument will mark their resting place—no epitaph will recount their talents and virtues for the instruction of succeeding generations—the hand of affection will not deck their graves with Flora's tributes—they sleep in ocean depths, awaiting the final judgment, when the sea shall give up its dead, and dust return to the God that gave it.

The public mind was altogether unprepared for the shock. Although the Arctic was anxiously looked for, no one thought that so stout and good a ship had met with any disaster. The consequence was that when we announced the terrible news, the metropolis assumed the appearance of one great funeral. This feeling spread through all classes of the community. The business streets, usually so gay and bustling, were filled with little groups of men, whose solemn countenances showed that they were fully impressed with the belief that no common disaster had befallen the city. In the home circle, the matter was talked over in whispers, and everywhere was expressed the deepest regret at the occurrence and the most profound sympathy for the relatives and friends of those on board.

The feeling extended beyond those who had any relatives, friends or acquaintances, for the Collins steamships are the pride and glory of New York, and our citizens regard their triumphs or their defeats—their safety or their dangers—as those of the city itself. This will account for the great depression which could be seen everywhere in the city yesterday. It is beyond description. It appeared that a great pall had been lowered upon us, and that everything was over-shadowed by its gloom.

The reporters did not rest. They sought out additional survivors and reinterviewed others for more details. A new dispatch arrived from Halifax, clicking down the telegraph wires all the way to New York by way of Boston. It stated the steamship that collided with *Arctic* was the French propeller *Vesta*. This new intelligence quashed the rumor that the liner had hit and sunk a troop ship bound for the Crimea and ignited yet another rumor that *Vesta* had rescued thirty-one more *Arctic* survivors. *Vesta* had limped into St. John's, Newfoundland, early on the morning of September 30. The watertight forward compartment held fast, and after it was reinforced, the ship's master brought her home, just missing the full brunt of the gale that blew up late Friday night on September 29. Had she not made port when she did, the storm probably would have sunk her.

The testimony of several of the crewmen, including Patrick Tobbin, created the first major stir of controversy. A subheadline on the front page of the *Herald* read: "Heartless Conduct of Some of the Officers and Crew of the Arctic." The emotions of many in the city, particularly those who had lost family and friends, swung rapidly from abject grief and despair to a cold, almost violent rage. That fury increased as the days went on and the headlines became harsher in their judgment of the crew. They were soon referred to as "dastardly" and "cowards" and "cruel" beyond words. The *New York Daily Times* voiced its opinion that the escape of the sailors and firemen in the boats, and the fact that many of them survived, was as "deplorable as the loss of Arctic" in the tragic consequences of the collision.

Throughout the coming weeks, the story continued to occupy the front pages of all the newspapers in New York and in the papers of other big cities across the United States. When news of the disaster reached Liverpool, the major newspapers in England and France carried the story as well. The *Times* of London asserted that the "passengers were drowned through the desertion of the crew."

On Friday, October 13, thirty-eight of the men in the two boats that made it to Newfoundland arrived back in New York, and the reception they received was hardly one of joy. By this time, the residents of the city knew all too well how these men managed to survive while so many others had died. Perhaps fearing just such a response or the possibility of criminal charges, six sailors chose to remain in Canada, adding to those who had elected to remain aboard *Huron*, which arrived on the same day in Quebec. Some of these sailors and firemen also chose not to return to New York, or indeed, to the United States. They disappeared on the waterfronts along the St. Lawrence River and found the obscurity they wanted.

There were still many who hoped the three missing boats might turn up or that news might reach the city of survivors plucked from the sea in the way McCabe and Dorian had found salvation aboard *Huron*. Those hopes were in part rewarded. Unknown to all those following the story and clinging to hope that their loved ones might still live, far up north on the swift-flowing tides of the St. Lawrence River estuary *Cambria* slowly made her way toward Quebec with her freight of *Arctic*'s last remaining survivors. Like *Huron*, she too put in to the quarantine station at the outskirts of Quebec on Friday evening, October 13, where she waited for official clearance to proceed to her berth.

In Captain Russell's private stateroom the following morning, James C. Luce began to write the report he would send via telegraph to Edward Knight Collins. He wrote slowly, choosing his words with care. But no matter how he expressed himself, the horror of the facts was inescapable.

CHAPTER NINETEEN

RESURRECTION

S UNLIGHT SPARKLED on the dark waters of the St. Lawrence River
and bathed the old city of Quebec in an early morning display of
reds merged with the cobalt blue of the northern sky. The light passed
through the portholes of Captain Russell's stateroom and illuminated
the pages of Luce's report spread out in front of him on the small desk
in the cabin. Luce blotted each sheet of paper to rid it of any excess ink
and prepared to reread the text a final time before going ashore to the
telegraph office. Later in the afternoon, he and his companions were to
catch a steamboat bound for Montreal and from there make their way
to New York by train and coach. He sighed and read the first lines:

Quebec. October 14, 1854
E. K. Collins—

Dear Sir—It becomes my painful duty to inform you of the
total loss of the Arctic, under my command, with many lives, and
I fear among them must be included your own wife, daughter,
and son, of whom I took a last leave the moment the ship was
going down, without ever expecting to see the light of another
day to give you an account of the heart-rending scene. . . .

Luce trembled as he came to the part of his report involving
Willie's death. The image of the paddle-wheel box flying up from the
depths and falling on top of his son was still so vivid it was as if the very
minute of the tragedy had just passed. He had dreamed of that mo-

ment. He realized that the images would remain with him. He assumed the sinking of *Arctic* terminated his career. As captain, he was solely responsible for the events that had transpired, and he would accept that responsibility. Life was uncertain in ways he had failed to understand as fully as he did now.

Luce reached the end of the report. The last two paragraphs announced his intentions and yet one more way he had tried faithfully to carry out his duty to his employer and the loved ones of the dead:

I have safely arrived at Quebec, and I am left without a penny in the world with which to help myself. With sincere gratitude to those from whom I have received such unbounded kindness since I have been providentially thrown amongst them, I am about to separate to go to New York—a home of sorrow.

I learned from the Doctor, at quarantine, last evening, that the Vesta had reached St. Johns with several passengers from the Arctic, but could not learn the particulars. As soon as I can get on shore I shall make arrangements to leave for New York with the least possible delay.

I take the steamer for Montreal this afternoon.

I am, very respectfully,
Your obedient servant,
James C. Luce

Luce gathered up the papers, tapped the ends of the pages on the desk to straighten them, and carefully folded the report into thirds, making it a long white rectangle. He placed it in the chest pocket of the jacket Captain Russell had given him, his own tattered and blood-soaked clothes long since relegated to the trash heap. He lightly touched the gash on his forehead and winced with pain. The wound would heal but never disappear. He would see the scar in the mirror every time he combed his hair in readiness for the new day.

He stood up and slowly crossed the stateroom to the door. He hesitated a moment, wanting to prolong the private time away from the men busy on deck offloading *Cambria*'s cargo. The sun cast shadows in the room. Despite the fire burning in the little iron stove, he felt chilled. He lifted the latch, opened the door, and stepped into the companionway. Gently, he pulled the door closed behind him and went up on deck to say good-bye to the man to whom he owed his life, the man who had shown him such kindness. He knew something of Captain Russell.

Almost two years ago, on December 4, 1852, Russell had endured the tragic loss of a command, *Jesse Stevens*. While on his way to Glasgow, a fierce midocean gale pounded the ship to pieces. He had fought hard to save her and the people aboard, but despite his efforts, she sank. Out of the storm, just before she went down, emerged the Collins liner *Pacific*, under command of Ezra Nye. The steamer hove to and sent lifeboats to the battered hulk. At great peril to his own crew, Captain Nye saved every man aboard *Jesse Stevens*. Russell told Luce the story during their two weeks together as *Cambria* sailed on to Quebec. Although Russell could not fully comprehend the true magnitude of Luce's misery and grief, like any other commander who had faced death and survived, he did have an inkling, a grasp of its extent, and for that Luce was grateful. It made him feel somehow less adrift and alone.

Russell nodded grimly as Luce made his way to him on the poop deck. They exchanged a few words. Before taking his leave, Luce took Russell's hand in his. "Thank you for all you have done," he said, and joined the other survivors waiting for him on the dock.

George Allen stood among the survivors looking as sad as any man might who had learned of the deaths of his family and friends. The newspapers in Quebec had picked up the stories published in New York. Peter McCabe's testimony about the events on the raft confirmed that Grace had lived only a few hours at most, that she had died with the rest of the Brown party. All were dead save him alone. He wondered why he had been spared while the rest had perished. The more sensitive of the survivors entertained the same thoughts, but others did not wonder at all. They attributed the random nature of life to God's will and left it at that, or did not consider their survival as anything more than a lucky break bestowed upon them at the expense of others who were weaker and incapable of fighting for the right to live. The strong always won out at sea. It was simply the way of it, part of a natural order.

In spite of his grief, his desire to turn inward into himself and withdraw from the painful reality he faced, Allen befriended the young German boy whom Luce and he had saved from suicide in his moment of despair. He offered Ferdinand Keyn a job at the Novelty Iron Works and a little money to get him on his feet. He, Keyn, Luce, and a handful of other survivors walked to the telegraph offices. Those who wished to sent messages to loved ones saying they were safe.

At the pier, the Montreal-bound steamer prepared for departure. The men of *Arctic* boarded and gazed at the water of the river, the city, the trees on the far shore. At last, the deckhands cast off the steamer's lines, and with a shriek from its steam whistle and a churning of its wheels, the vessel got under way. She reached Montreal later that afternoon and came to rest at her berth at the edge of the bustling city roughly five hundred miles from the sea, just below the thundering Lachine Rapids. Oceangoing ships lined the stone quays. Stevedores and longshoremen finished up the last of the day's work transferring the cargo to smaller vessels bound for Lake Ontario by way of the Lachine Canal built in 1825 to create a passage around the whitewater tumbling downriver past the limestone commercial buildings on the waterfront.

Upon their arrival in Montreal, the three-day journey began in earnest. The passengers made their way to the train depot and embarked on the evening express, the first leg of a trip involving several connections to various railroads that led finally to the Hudson River. Once there, the men would ride south along the river's edge home to Manhattan on the Albany Express. The night train rolled out of the station under a cloud of burning red wood cinders showering the top of the cars. The cinders glowed as they flew back along the sides of the train and blinked out when they settled on the stones of the rail bed. Luce watched them. They looked like little stars that brightened the blackness of the world.

The report that Luce sent arrived in New York while he traveled up the St. Lawrence River on the steamer to Montreal. The courier rushed the dispatch to Edward Knight Collins, putting to rest the rumors circulating that his wife, daughter, and son might have survived. Collins's despair was complete. The newspapers got hold of Luce's report and the following day, Sunday, October 15, it made front-page news. The brave captain lived! The people of the city rejoiced, including Elizabeth. A deeply religious woman, she considered the news with the mixed emotions natural for anyone in her position. God had taken the only child she would ever bring into the world, but had spared the only man she ever would love.

Luce's train rattled westward down through the forests of Canada and New England at twenty miles per hour. Throughout Sunday, crowds gathered at every stop to pay their respects to Captain Luce, whom they considered a hero. The men stood with their hats held over their chests, the women with their heads bowed. Sometimes the crowds cheered, but more often they remained silent. People gathered even in stations where the train did not stop, demonstrating their solidarity and sympathy for him. The sight was both gratifying and upsetting to Luce and those with him.

On Sunday morning, the *New York Herald* covered a special service held at the Episcopal church in Yonkers, of which Elizabeth Fearing Luce was a parishioner, to mourn the dead and celebrate the living. The *Herald* reported:

> When the news of the loss of the Arctic reached Yonkers, the residence of Captain Luce's family, every one felt as if a dear friend had been swept from their midst. Whatever hopes

might have been entertained of the safety of any one on board the ill-fated vessel, even the most sanguine never thought for an instant that her commander would be rescued. He had been seen on the deck when she sank, and those who had been with him but a few minutes before, asserted it as their positive belief that he had perished with her. The news when brought to his wife threw her into the most profound grief, but who can express the intense joy which she felt on receiving the glad intelligence that he whom every one believed to be dead was alive, and that in a day or two more she would again welcome him to his home?

The loss of his son and many of his friends will cast a shade over their meeting. . . .

Late in the afternoon of Monday, October 16, Luce and his companions reached Troy on the Northern rail line only a half-hour before the Albany Express left for New York City at five o'clock. As the train pulled into the station, Luce glanced out the soot-coated window and saw a crowd of two thousand people standing on the platform and in the nearby streets. As he hurried with the others out of the train, a tremendous shout greeted him. The crowd rushed toward him, the men shaking his hand and wishing him well. It was intimidating and brought back memories of the panicked throng rushing him aboard *Arctic*. He received the thanks of the well-wishers as cordially as possible, but he tried to get away from them as quickly as he could.

"[Luce] was overwhelmed with the congratulations of the assembled friends who rushed upon him, to grasp him by the hand and congratulate him for his safe deliverance from the perils of the deep. Having no time to wait, the gallant captain could do no more than simply thank his various friends for their interest in his safety," wrote a reporter for the *Herald* who witnessed the scene.

Luce and his companions made their way to the depot for the Albany Express and found gathered there another crowd, somewhat smaller but perhaps even more enthusiastic. "Nine cheers for the gallant tar who would not desert his ship!" a man yelled. "Nine cheers!" Immediately, the crowd began cheering wildly.

The train pulled away. The voices of the cheering multitude drowned out the hoot of the whistle, the clack and squeak of the wheels on the track. The noise grew fainter as the train moved farther away, until the din faded completely:

> At every stopping place along the line of the railroad the same scene was enacted. At some places where the cars did not stop, hundreds were assembled to give him three cheers as he passed by. At Hudson there was a very large meeting, and the rush into the cars to get a glimpse at the rescued commander, soon crowded them from the locomotive to the rear car. All appeared to be mad with delight at the preservation and return of him who resolved "To stand by his vessel till she sunk."

At last the train approached Yonkers. It was nine-thirty in the evening and as dark as the inside of a top hat. Yet the town was lit up with lanterns, presenting a peculiarly cheerful ambiance. Every window seemed to glow with flickering yellow light, warm and inviting in the cold autumn air. Luce stood up to go. George Allen stood up to say good-bye to his friend; he and Keyn were continuing on to New York.

> The public heart bleeds in sympathy with [Allen], who returns so sadly to his home, leaving his wife, child, and many relatives buried in the sea.

Luce shook his friend's hand. He stared at Allen and saw the blank look of emptiness. The life seemed to have gone out of his eyes. His face was gaunt and haggard. "Good night, George," Luce said. "I will see you tomorrow when I come down to the city."

Allen squeezed Luce's hand and slumped back in his seat next to Keyn.

Luce walked slowly down the aisle of the car, braced for the same well-meant but out-of-place jubilance he had endured for almost the entire trip home. He reached the door of the car and looked out at the crowd of hundreds gathered there to welcome him. Not one person cheered. They silently formed two long lines. Several men walked toward him between the line of spectators. He recognized his close friend, Judge Wordworth, and others. They stopped in front of him. Luce stepped down from the train worn out from it all.

"Welcome home, Captain," Wordworth said, clasping his hand in his. "Come. Elizabeth is waiting for you."

With his friends at his side, Luce walked between the two lines of people, the men with their hats clutched to their chests. In the dull light of the lanterns, Luce could see tears streaming down many faces. Everyone remained silent out of respect for him. At the end of the line, a carriage waited. He and his closest friends got in. The driver flicked the reins, and the horses began to move at a slow walk. The crowd followed, surrounding the carriage. The lights from the lanterns swayed as the men carrying them walked on, casting shadows at one moment and illuminating the somber faces of the men and women at another. The carriage stopped in front of his home. The crowd stayed back.

Luce and those with him in the carriage stepped out. He took a long look at the men and women who had come to show their feelings of friendship and sympathy. "Thank you," he said, then turned away from them and walked to the house. The front door opened and there stood Elizabeth. She took him gently by the hand and led him inside, closing the door behind her. Outside the house, the people walked silently back to their own homes.

CHAPTER TWENTY

AFTERMATH

HEADLINES AND STORIES related to the *Arctic* disaster occupied the front pages of the major New York newspapers through October 22, until coverage of the battles in the Crimea replaced them. Letters from outraged citizens condemned the actions of the crewmen, who in turn gave additional statements to the press in an effort to justify their actions. The following sequence of statements from Third Officer Francis Dorian and Second Officer William Baalham are illustrative of the tone of the reports.

On October 13, Francis Dorian stated in the *New York Herald* that "if the officers and men had remained by the ship, all or nearly all of the passengers would have been saved." Dorian's assertion was correct. But that would have meant the crew had to sacrifice their own lives for the people in their care, something they did not wish to do, even if the law said they must. This stands in stark contrast to the actions of the crew aboard *Titanic* fifty-eight years later.

The next day, Second Officer William Baalham responded to Dorian's assertion. He said: "The question may be asked, 'why is it that so large a proportion of those who were saved were of the crew, and so few of the passengers?'" Indeed, this was the prevailing question of the day. Baalham continued, "The answer is this—the order was given me by Captain Luce to jump into the boat; and this I did, accompanied by three others. We were the only persons in the boat when the falls were cut by order of the Captain, and the boat struck the water. The sea was filled with human beings, many of whom had jumped overboard, and all of them struggling for life. Their wild shrieks for help were heartrending; we did not stop to see who wore broadcloth [dresses] or red shirts, but went to work with all haste to pick up the poor wretches, and we soon filled our boat."

Baalham neglected to say that Captain Luce had ordered him to go astern, away from the crewmen leaping over the side in their frantic attempt to get into the boat, where he might take on women and children. Other testimony also indicates that the boat was not completely filled when Baalham allowed it to drift away from the ship. It should be noted that Baalham thought Captain Luce was dead, as did the rest of the world. Without Captain Luce alive to contradict him, Baalham was able to fashion his statements to put himself in the best light. News of Luce's rescue did not break until October 15 and when it did, Luce expressed his shock over Baalham's actions.

As the evil of the crew became increasingly evident, the public outcry grew more intense, though by modern standards it was quite mild. A letter dated October 18, addressed to the editor of the *New York Daily Times*, said:

> Sir: I have noticed in your truly valuable journal many comments on the heartless desertion of the crew at the very time when they were most needed on the ill-fated Arctic. Now, Sir, according to my judgment, public sentiment should go still further, and expose these craven-hearted (men?) to the scorn of the world in a way they would not soon forget. My plan is this: Let the names of the crew of the Arctic who so basely deserted their trust be conspicuously posted in every shipping office in the City, and whenever a man presents himself for a place, let the agent see if his name be on the proscribed list; if so, let him say . . . "We want no such men on our ships." I do not propose this as a petty revenge, but in order that if at any future time our wives or children should be absent upon the broad Atlantic [these men will not be able to repeat what they did aboard Arctic].

Although there were laws on the books that stated crewmen must, in the event of an emergency, give passengers seats in the lifeboats before attempting to save themselves, not one man was charged with a crime. The letter quoted above represents the harshest call for action against the men. It must be remembered that the mid-1850s in America were rough-and-tumble times, and far less litigious than the present. The crewmen were publicly disgraced. That seemed to be enough punishment and the public quickly turned its attention to other areas, some quite appropriate for focus.

Some of the letters questioned whether Captain Luce had asserted himself enough to impose sufficient discipline. Luce's hero status faded as public sentiment in certain quarters turned against him and the Collins Line for its "wicked recklessness of speed" in all weather and circumstances at sea. People conveniently forgot the headlines about how superior America was to Great Britain, that Edward Knight Collins had indeed "cast this man Cunard from the sea" because of the exceptional speed and luxury of the steamers he built to compete with his rival. They did not excuse Luce for acting in accordance with the practice of every packet ship master.

Attention to the grave dangers of proceeding on at top speed in all weather and when icebergs were present on the Grand Banks was short-lived. The issue soon fell dormant, and the popularity of steamers that made the fastest passages quickly rose again. Ships did not slow down in the fog or when icebergs loomed over the horizon. The competition between Great Britain and the United States went on unabated, at least for a few more years.

Editorials called for increased safety measures, stating the obvious fact that steamships sailing under the flag of the United States in the transatlantic trade should carry enough lifeboats for every man, woman, and child, as well as all of the crew in the event of an emergency. Collins did add five boats to each of his remaining three ships, and Cunard added boats to his ships as well. However, steamers continued to leave port without enough boats for every person aboard, though they were equipped with the legal number under the law, just as *Arctic* was when she sank.

Fifty-eight years later, the British ship *Titanic*, carrying the legal number of boats, once again illustrated that sufficient laws were not yet in place to ensure a seat in a lifeboat for an entire ship's company. Those in charge of *Titanic* also failed to attend to basic safety measures and sped their flagship, like *Arctic*, through dangerous waters seemingly without concern. The same competitive impulses existed among the shipowners in 1912 as they did in 1854, as each company sought the glory that came with the fastest sailing times across the ocean in the Great Atlantic Race that went on well into the twentieth century.

The editorials following the sinking of *Arctic* called for the precaution of provisioning the lifeboats with food and water for two weeks, which typically was not done because it cost the shipowners too much money. *Arctic*'s boats were not provisioned, nor did they have compasses aboard. Proposals that the crews train for abandon-ship situations, with every man assigned a post of duty, also came up, as did suggestions that all ships should have steam whistles and all masters should use them when visibility was limited. None of these reforms was immediately adopted. It took time, and more people drowned as a result.

After the story moved to the back pages of the newspapers and disappeared altogether, hope lingered on that some survivors may have been picked up on outbound ships or that the lifeboats might still appear. Gradually, though, the loved ones with missing family and friends gave up hope. In mid-November, the lifeboat that First Officer Robert Gourlay had taken to assist *Vesta* was discovered empty and adrift on the Grand Banks. All the oars were still inside and the boat was in good condition. Again, hopes arose that the faithful first mate and his six companions had been rescued by an outbound ship. But the bleak reality indicated that it was far more likely the men were all dead. As each man starved to death or died of exposure, his body was thrown overboard, until the last of the men committed suicide in a fit of despair and delirium, leaping into the ocean to end his misery. Gourlay and his men were never heard from again.

In December, another of *Arctic*'s lifeboats was found washed ashore in Newfoundland. No bodies were discovered. The whereabouts of the third lifeboat remained a mystery. The sea had swallowed it up, along with Chief Engineer J. W. Rogers and his fellow deserters. Approximately fifty people escaped from *Arctic* in the three missing boats. Thinking themselves safe, their lives were still lost.

The total number of *Arctic* survivors, excluding Jassonet François of *Vesta*, who was picked up with Luce and the others, amounted to the thirty-one men in Francis Dorian's boat, Peter McCabe on the raft, the forty-five men in the two boats that made it to Newfoundland, and the nine men saved aboard *Cambria*. Of the eighty-six survivors, only twenty-two of them were passengers. Jassonet François, possibly the luckiest man involved in the disaster, also saved aboard *Cambria*, brought the total number of survivors to eighty-seven.

The exact number of people aboard *Arctic* is unknown, in part because extra crewmen were hired in Liverpool and Luce's record of them went down with the ship. Captain Luce's initial report stated that there were 238 passengers and about 150 crewmen aboard *Arctic* when she set out from Liverpool, for a total of 388 people. This total may not have accounted for Luce's son, Luce himself, and his officers.

On October 17, the *New York Herald* published the following breakdown of all those who sailed in *Arctic*. It differs from the numbers listed in Luce's report and does not count Willie or Jassonet François. It may also not classify teenage passengers as children, and it does not indicate the gender of the servants or that of passengers' friends. A good number of the servants and friends were female:

Passengers

Men	128
Women	58
Children	22
Persons designated as passengers' friends	17
Servants and nurses	8
Total	*233*

Crew

Men	168
Women	2
Boys	5
Total	*175*

Total on board	*408*

These figures reveal the nature of the shipwreck in stark terms without the abundant testimony of the survivors. The best estimates available state that *Arctic*'s six lifeboats were capable of carrying about 180 people, or nearly all the passengers and certainly all the women and children. The fact that only twenty-two of the strongest, most agile male passengers lived through the disaster shows the extent of the horror that must have taken place aboard the liner in the ship's final hours. Even without the abundant first-hand testimony from survivors, these figures speak for themselves. The events surrounding *Arctic*'s loss on Wednesday, September 27, 1854, haunted Captain Luce for the rest of his life.

Luce never went to sea again as a captain. Instead, he pursued a new career that focused on safety issues regarding maritime commerce. He became what in modern terms is known as a marine surveyor—an inspector of ships to ensure that they met all the requirements for safe operation under the law. He went to work for the Great Western Marine Insurance Company and continued his employment at the firm until his death. He and Elizabeth endured yet more misfortune. In 1858, Robert died of consumption at the age of twenty-one while finishing up his last year of college. After the death of their only remaining son, Luce sold the house in Yonkers. He and his wife moved to New Rochelle and built a "handsome residence" there. Together, he and Elizabeth passed the years they had left.

On Wednesday evening, July 9, 1879, Luce left work at the insurance company a little early, saying he did not feel well. He was getting on in years, having celebrated his seventy-fourth birthday in April. "For several years past [he] had been in rather delicate health, though never failing in his attention to business. He was in comfortable circumstances, and well liked by the people of New Rochelle, a place to which he was very much attached," according to the *Herald*. On his way back to New Rochelle, "he was taken with a fit of retching and went to bed" as soon as he arrived home. Worried about her husband, Elizabeth called a doctor. "A drink was given him at night, and he appeared to be all right again, but the next moment he turned over on his side and expired without a note of warning."

His obituary, published in the *New York Times* on July 11, 1879, said he "lived to see many more years of active life [after *Arctic* sank], although his later years were embittered by the recollection of the terrible disaster in which several hundred persons lost their lives—a disaster, however, for which he was in no way responsible. . . . His associates say he never went to sleep afterward, without a vision of the terrible catastrophe before his mind." The obituary in the *New York Herald* also mentioned Luce's haunting, saying Luce "lost his son . . . to whom he was devotedly attached and of whom he never ceased to think till the day of his death."

After forty-one years of marriage to the only man she ever loved, Elizabeth was left a widow. She dressed in black and stayed at his side while a procession of friends and associates came to the house to pay their respects. The funeral was held Friday evening, and the next day she accompanied the body of her husband to Center Cemetery in Wareham, Massachusetts. He was placed in a vault belonging to her family. Nearby were Robert's grave and a stone pillar erected in memory of Willie. The inscription read: WILLIE FEARING LUCE. DIED AT SEA 1854. AGED 11 YEARS.

Other families built monuments and memorials to honor the memory of their loved ones. James Brown, president of the Collins Line, erected a grand monument in Greenwood Cemetery in Brooklyn. Although its spires and Gothic decorations are much eroded from the effects of the elements, visitors to the site more than a century later can still make out the names carved at the base of the pedestal of the six members of the Brown family who died aboard *Arctic*. Atop the pedestal is a sculpture of *Arctic* herself, caught in the process of sinking beneath the waves, her bow uplifted, the waters meeting across her upper deck.

George Allen, the only member of the Brown party to survive, spoke of the events that occurred aboard *Arctic* just once, according to family records obtained by the late Alexander Crosby Brown, great-grandson of James Brown, president of the Collins Line. Allen made his family promise to never speak of the wreck in his presence, and he evidently suffered from survivor's guilt. Shortly after his return to New York City with Captain Luce, he sobbed as he told the story of what had happened and questioned why he was spared while the rest of his loved ones had died. As the ship sank, all of the Browns, and Allen and his wife, Grace, decided that if one of them was to live, it should be Millie, the favorite daughter of James Brown. Allen reportedly held Millie's hand, while Grace held the infant Herbert, but at the last moment Grace begged Allen to save their baby. Allen was sucked down with the ship, and the force of the water ripped Herbert from Allen's arms. Allen died on August 29, 1863. Photographs of him prior to his death show a gaunt, haunted face.

Allen befriended Ferdinand Keyn, the German sailor, who worked for Novelty Iron Works, in which the Allens held an interest. But the sea drew him back to it. He served in the German merchant marine and rose to the rank of captain. In 1876, while master of the ship *Fran-*

conia, Keyn's vessel collided with a British steamship in the English Channel. Like Luce, he lost his position.

Edward Knight Collins mourned for his wife and two children. However, the press of business brought him out of seclusion. Fortunately for him and other major stockholders in the company, there was no widespread panic about the safety of the remaining Collins steamers. They were more crowded than ever, in part because the fleet's carrying capacity was reduced by 25 percent. *Arctic* and her cargo were well insured, which helped lessen the immediate financial liabilities for the company. Yet the ship's loss set the stage for the firm's ultimate demise, and it can be argued that it stopped the Collins Line from surpassing the Cunard Line when the British company was unusually vulnerable. Red ink still colored the ledgers even more than in the past; after all, four ships could generate more cash than three. Moreover, the loss of initiative in private investment and the reduction of congressional subsidies in the wake of such disaster is incalculable.

A year later, world events added to the pressure building against the solvency of the Collins Line. In September 1855, the fortified Russian naval base at Sevastopol in the Crimea fell, and the French, Turks, and British put the Russian Army on the run. The war lurched into its final phase as the year ended. As the troop ships came home to England and were converted back into liners, Samuel Cunard began to reassert his influence on the transatlantic trade. He had already initiated plans to build the finest ship in his line to put up against the ships of the Collins fleet. She was *Persia*, the first iron steamship of the Cunard Line, and the largest at 3,766 tons gross register and 350 feet along the keel. Her engines could develop up to 3,600 horsepower to drive her through the seas.

True to the character of their ongoing rivalry, Edward Knight Collins launched plans of his own to outdo Samuel Cunard once again. He raised cash from his now-wary backers, over $1 million, to fund the construction of his biggest liner yet, the largest ship ever built in the United States up to that time. She was *Adriatic*, designed by

George Steers and built under his direct supervision in his shipyard at the foot of Seventh Street in New York. *Adriatic* was 354 feet in length and 3,670 tons gross register. Her two engines were capable of developing 2,800 horsepower. She was built of wood, but at the request of Edward Knight Collins, Steers fitted her interior with watertight compartments. (As soon as it was possible, the other Collins ships had also been equipped with watertight compartments after the *Arctic* disaster.)

On both sides of the Atlantic, the race to build the biggest and best ocean liners continued. To all appearances, it was business as usual. Cunard, however, soon pulled ahead. He was the first to launch his latest creation, and *Persia* was in operation by early 1856.

The Collins Line was hard pressed, and the fortunes of the company were about to suffer yet another blow. Sailing under command of Ezra Nye, with 141 crewmen and only 45 passengers aboard, *Pacific* set out from Liverpool on January 23, 1856. She steamed directly into one of the worst ice fields a ship ever encountered and disappeared without a trace. It is uncertain just how she was lost, but the evidence suggests she encountered the same ice reported by *Persia*, which some sources say damaged her after she sailed a few days subsequent to the departure of *Pacific*. The ship *Edinburgh* also reported the ice field and spotted wreckage that looked as if it might have come off the missing Collins liner.

This second disaster hit Collins hard. *Adriatic* was not yet ready for service, and *Baltic* and *Atlantic* could simply not do the work of four vessels. It seemed all might end badly for Collins. Yet he battled on. British shipping merchant W. S. Lindsay provided a description of this American spirit from his perspective:

> These terrible disasters [the loss of *Arctic* and *Pacific*] did not, however, quench the spirit of the American people, however much they may have grieved over them. They were still as resolved as ever to maintain an Atlantic mail service of their

own, and the requisite capital was soon found to supply the place of the two vessels which had been lost; one of the new steamers, the *Adriatic*, surpassing in size, speed, and splendour any of her predecessors. Nor did these disasters check the passenger traffic which, in eight years from the time of starting the Collins line, had increased five-fold.

On April 7, 1856, more than 60,000 spectators gathered in the shipyard of George Steers to witness the launching of *Adriatic*. It was deemed one of the most well-attended launches in the United States during this period of maritime history. The hopes of all concerned with the Collins Line rested on this ship. Cunard for the first time had drawn solidly ahead in the Great Atlantic Race since the first Collins ships put to sea back in 1850. It was hoped that *Adriatic* might tilt the odds back in favor of the Americans.

Delays in fitting *Adriatic* out for sea, partly due to the untimely death of George Steers not long after the ship was launched, exacerbated the dire financial condition of the company. In addition, the detractors opposed to the continued subsidy from the U.S. Treasury, particularly given the sorry state of the fleet in 1856, gained power and influence in the halls of Congress. By February 1857, Congress had cut the annual subsidy back to its original $385,000, essentially dooming the Collins Line to bankruptcy as its creditors sought payment of outstanding bills in increasing number and with increasing zeal. Part of the worry of the creditors was linked to a national depression, the panic of 1857, that had been building since the mid-1850s and finally exploded in a market collapse that shook the country to its very foundations.

W. S. Lindsay wrote of the final days of the Collins Line:

In a comparative statement of the voyages of the principal steamers then engaged in the Transatlantic trade, including the Collins line, the average speed of the Cunarders throughout the year 1856 exceeded that of all others; the *Persia* during that year having, on four occasions, made the passage from New York to Liverpool in less than nine days and a half, indeed, in one instance, in nine days, four hours, and thirty-five minutes.

But the Collins Company continued to run their ships with regularity and undaunted vigour up till 1858, and it was only when the shareholders discovered that they were competing with the Cunard and other British steamers at a ruinous loss, and declined to provide more capital, that this great but spirited undertaking was relinquished. Though the most strenuous exertions were made, every effort failed to resuscitate the Company. The losses had been stupendous: minor and separate interests, moreover, as well as those persons who, from the first, had been opposed to subsidies for the conveyance of the mails, now brought their influence to bear upon Congress.

The merchants and shipowners of Boston, Philadelphia, Baltimore, and other places, envious of New York, complained loudly of that city having a virtual monopoly of the Transatlantic trade, nor did the owners of the sailing packets fail to renew their protests against the large annual grants of public money voted for ocean steam communication. In the face of these remonstrances, and of the numerous hostile interests now at work, the American Government declined to grant any further subsidies to the Collins Company, or to aid, from the public purse, another undertaking which proposed to take its place.

Adriatic made only one voyage. She sailed in November 1857 and was laid up upon her return. The grand undertaking, which had held little promise of financial reward given the costs involved in the operation and the prevailing profit margins, ended on April 1, 1858, when

Adriatic, Baltic, and *Atlantic* were auctioned off for a mere $50,000. Edward Knight Collins got out of the shipping business for good. Like Captain Luce, he had had his fill of the sea. He now concentrated on developing coal and iron enterprises on properties he owned in Ohio, with modest success. He spent his final years in his home on Madison Avenue in New York and died on January 22, 1878, at the age of seventy-five.

In just a decade, between 1848 and 1858, the U.S. merchant marine achieved its peak of greatness and subsequently lost its position of prominence, as Britain, France, and Germany surged ahead in the transatlantic steamship trade. The packets continued to sail, but the profits of the past were no longer available to the Yankee owners and captains. The swift clipper ships came and went, and gradually disappeared altogether. The fast and luxurious steamships that were once the pride of the nation vanished into oblivion, at least for a time. The United States turned inward and put her back to the sea. The young men who sought their fortunes on the poop decks of sailing vessels looked westward for their chance at the American dream.

But that decade had brought glory days to the American experience, the pomp and vigor of a newly formed country still in the process of establishing a national identity. They marked one of the most important chapters of America's development in business and technology in the nineteenth century and so helped set the stage for its ultimate rise as a major international power. Yet, lest we forget, beneath these technological advances and business enterprises lie victims of progress, souls the sea has claimed for its own.

AUTHOR'S NOTE

HISTORICAL NARRATIVE depends on its primary documents, eye-witness accounts, newspaper reports, and other materials. The story of *Arctic* has a plenitude of such documents to draw on. However, a close study of all the material available inevitably turns up discrepancies, an incorrect date here and there, an error of fact or a somewhat slanted interpretation. I did my best to cull through the sources and compare them against each other to arrive at the most objective and accurate presentation of the facts possible.

Especially helpful sources were the *New York Herald, New York Daily Times, Harper's New Monthly Magazine,* and *History of Merchant Shipping and Ancient Commerce* by W. S. Lindsay, a British merchant writing in the 1870s who provided the perspective of an Englishman on the competition between Samuel Cunard and Edward Knight Collins. The American publications were understandably biased in favor of Collins.

A more recent source of great help in writing this book was *Women and Children Last*. Appropriately titled, this is a careful study of the *Arctic* disaster published in 1961 by Alexander Crosby Brown, great-grandson of James Brown. On the workings of New York Harbor and the rise of the New York packets, Robert Greenhalgh Albion's *The Rise of New York Port, 1815–1860* and *Square-Riggers on Schedule* were also valuable. Additional sources are listed in the Bibliography.

Readers will note that the chapters leading up to the shipwreck contain little or no dialogue. As the events surrounding the collision, the sinking, and its aftermath unfold, the dialogue increases. The first-hand testimony printed in the newspapers of the day included direct quotations of what witnesses said during the shipwreck, which I sometimes included in my story. Survivors also reported the dialogue other passengers had spoken during the shipwreck, and I frequently quoted them. Finally, I sometimes provide the direct testimony. No dialogue of my own invention appears in my text.

Although the story may seem surprisingly detailed at times, no details were invented. For example, just before the collision occurred, readers will note *Arctic* rises up on a wave and meets *Vesta* in the trough. This kind of observation was not imagined but came from eyewitnesses.

A novel could not readily accommodate the twists and turns of coincidence and serendipity that the story of *Arctic* presents. Yet they were true and confirmed by more than one witness. Of all the people thrashing in the water after the ship sank, among those to climb on Peter McCabe's raft were most of the Brown party save for George Allen's son, Herbert, and William and Clara Brown's daughter, who had drowned moments earlier. Only four of the people aboard the raft were women, all from the Brown party. Two credible witnesses confirm that this happened—Captain Luce and second-class passenger James Smith.

On October 18, Luce's report in the *New York Herald* contained the following sentences: "After Mr. Allen and I had got upon the raft [paddle-wheel box], we saw Mrs. Allen, Mrs. Brown [William Brown's wife, Clara], Miss Maria Brown, William B. Brown and lady [most likely the nurse of William and Clara Brown's infant daughter, Grace Alice Jane], and some fifty others on the main raft; and they were still upon the raft when we last saw them."

On October 17, in the *New York Daily Times*, James Smith confirmed that the Brown party was on McCabe's raft, though he said they were put aboard before *Arctic* sank. This seems unlikely—given Patrick Tobbin's testimony, from his vantage point in Francis Dorian's lifeboat, stating that the unfinished raft got trapped beneath the starboard paddle-wheel box as the ship sank, killing most of those who had taken refuge there. Smith said: "Mr. Allen too, although saved himself has too much reason to fear the loss of his wife and several other relatives, who were on board [*Arctic*] with him and whom he saw placed on the raft of spars before the ship went under."

Of all people to save Jassonet François, it was Ferdinand Keyn, the German sailor who survived with Luce and Allen on the paddle-wheel box, and who owed his life to Jassonet François for informing the captain of *Cambria* about the presence of other survivors in the area when he was picked up. On October 18, in the *New York Herald*, the report from Luce included the following statement:

> After the collision with the *Vesta*, it will be remembered that a boat was sent from the *Vesta*, which was run over by the *Arctic*. Ferdinand Keyn, the young German who was saved on the piece of the wreck with Captain Luce and Mr. Allen, threw overboard a rope to one of the occupants of the boat, and by this act he was rescued. He proved to be a French fisherman. . . . Subsequently, when they were floating about on the ocean, in sight of the *Cambria*, and unable to attract attention from their extreme distance, this same fisherman chanced to float near to the *Cambria*, was discovered and picked up. Immediately upon going on board he intimated by signs that there were others on other pieces of wreck in the immediate vicinity, and this led to the rescue of Captain Luce and the others.
>
> It is thus seen that the act of Keyn in throwing a rope to the Frenchman was the means of preserving the lives, not only of the latter, but of Captain Luce, himself, Mr. Allen, and the few remaining survivors.

The details concerning the means by which the men of *Cambria* rescued Jassonet François were related to James Smith, and others. Smith's testimony in the *New York Daily Times* on October 17 stated:

I was surprised to learn that the old Frenchman who we had picked up from the *Vesta* was our good genius on this occasion. Being directly in the track of the approaching *Cambria*, he was picked up by the second mate of the *Cambria*, Mr. Ross, jumping overboard with a line, and, seizing hold of the old man, they were both pulled on board, and the rescued Frenchman, in the best English he could muster, made Capt. Russell aware that others were near, who then went to the masthead and with his glass made out the other four pieces of wreck, which we were all on, and making his long tack to windward came back in the midst of us, picking up first, from that half round piece of wreck that I saw burst above the surface at the time of the ship going under, Capt. Luce, Mr. George F. Allen, of the Novelty Works, and a young German, a passenger on the *Arctic*, by the name of Ferdinand Kaye [Keyn].

The sources of all the details contained in the text are akin to these. I am indebted to all of the witnesses and to the reporters who took such pains to record every detail ranging from the main events to the seemingly inconsequential. Without them, this book could not have been written.

However, one case where the testimony gets a bit muddy involves the chronology of when events occurred at the boats. This bears further explanation. Robert Gourlay's boat left first. It appears that the butcher's boat left second, but it is possible that the boat that toppled the passengers into the sea may have capsized before the butcher's boat left or at the same time. There are other similar questions too numerous to go through here. I compared all the testimony and based the narrative on a chronology borne out by more than one witness. The events recounted here concerning each boat have more than one witness reporting what happened, and their stories match. It is clear that Chief Engineer J. W. Rogers and his men stole the smallest boat and threatened several passengers with revolvers, though evidently not

James Smith. The bulk of the testimony is remarkably consistent, so much so that the *Herald* and the *Times* comment on this fact on more than one occasion.

On the two references to the supernatural in the narrative, Charles Mitchell, the cotton merchant from Charleston, told the newspapers that his sister Caroline had a premonition of evil the night of September 19 and refused to go aboard *Arctic*. Here again, the two lines of dialogue in the narrative are based on the testimony. The fortune-teller anecdote regarding William Brown at Barnum's came from a letter by Charles C. Nott, a friend of the Brown family, written on May 27, 1912, in his old age. The letter was addressed to Mrs. John Crosby Brown, a daughter-in-law of the late James Brown, former president of the Collins Line. Inspired by the recent *Titanic* disaster, Mrs. Brown evidently encouraged all those in her circle of family and friends to record their recollections of details associated with the loss of *Arctic* fifty-eight years earlier. Nott learned of the fortune-teller incident from his best friend, Howard Potter, who witnessed it and told Nott about it. He also reported exactly what the fortune-teller told Brown. There is no reason to doubt that the incident occurred, though some might wonder whether the fortune-teller really did have a premonition that William Brown would someday die in a shipwreck.

Nott also mentioned Millie Brown in his letter. When Nott read Peter McCabe's account of the events on the raft, he thought it possible that the last girl to die was Millie. She would have been seen with Luce at the captain's table and with him on deck, and Nott figured such a high-profile passenger might be known to McCabe. He decided to visit the young waiter on Staten Island, where he was recovering from his ordeal. But at the last moment, Nott changed his mind. He did not want to know. What good would the knowledge do?

The references to Millie's budding romance with William Gilbert were reported by the late Alexander Crosby Brown, based on family records and information he gleaned from relatives when he did his research nearly fifty years ago. Ironically, of all those in the Brown party, Millie was the least enthusiastic about the trip to Europe. Her parents did not want her to go, and they made George Allen promise to protect her, which may account for his initial decision to put her life above that of his son, Herbert.

APPENDIX: "THE LOSS OF THE ARCTIC"

THE WRECK OF STEAMSHIP ARCTIC touched all classes of people in New York City. Letters from readers expressing outrage at the actions of some of the crew and officers aboard the liner and deep sadness for the families of the victims flooded the major daily newspapers. On October 22, 1854, the following poem from an anonymous contributor appeared in the *New York Herald*. It is not great literature, but it reveals the emotion the shipwreck caused among the general public in a way that is especially emblematic of its time.

The Loss of the Arctic
By an anonymous contributor

The mist crouched on the ocean. Darkly speeds
    The gallant steamer on her well known way—
Her huge frame quivering as its circling wheels
    Urge the sharp prow through wave and milk-white spray.
Hundreds of hearts with joy and hope beat high
    To think their ocean road was well-nigh past;
And through their dreams the loves of "Fatherland,"
    And home, and all they prize, are fluttering fast.

Some were there who for the first time had left
    All which had once made life less chill and drear;
And some who hurried o'er the waves to join
    The cherished ones who made that life more dear—
Wives, who from husbands parted, sought their sides
    With kindling hope—children whose blooming years

Presaged a brighter growth—parental love
    Which found relief for parting in its tears.

A motley throng—some friends of those they left,
    And some dear friends of those to whom they sped,
Some from a pleasant journey wending home,
    Some, pilgrim-like, an unknown land to tread.
But the glad winds that sweep o'er God's broad world
    Had given all a joy; to all they told,
As the blue waves beneath their kisses leapt,
    Of pleasure, love, or wealth, of mirth or gold.

The mist slept on the waters. No one dreamed
    That, brooding darkly o'er the vessel's bow,
Fate hung in gloom, while death, with close veiled head,
    Crouched like a phantom on the pointed prow.
A gallant captain, and a crew who long
    Had trod and battled with the ocean wave,
Concealed the darkening shadows from their view,
    And made the veriest poltroon feel more brave.

And so the steamer sped upon her way,
    None imagined danger, till that danger came—
A shock, which quivered through from stem to stern,
    Shook the stout vessel's ribs and seasoned frame
Another—then, another. On the deck
    Raced from below, the dreamers. Through the gloom
A partial wreck is veering on the waves.
    As yet, unconscious of their hurrying doom.

The boat is hoisted out. The steersman's hand
    Obeys the captain. Answering to his will,
The steamer circles round the injured craft,
    The sailors ply their oars with a wonted skill,
But as they think of others, a fierce cry
    Rings from below. A shout of sudden fear
Rises athwart the decks, and smites its dread
    And terror on the listener's startled ear.

That shock has torn her timbers. Through them rush
　　The thirsty waters. Vainly, would they check
The angry torrent, which with restless sweep,
　　Gains, inch by inch upon the fireman's deck.
All is confusion. None who should have strength
　　To rule the crew in that most awful hour,
Retain the energy. A maddened fear
　　Usurps the will, and wields its selfish power.

Vain the commander's voice—In vain his words,
　　Whose spirit in that hour sublimed. They gave
A chance of safety—pushing it aside,
　　He bade them turn the helpless ones to save
Thrice noble youth! He now had found a home,
　　Young as he left that world in which he trod,
Beneath the will which gave his form a heart,
　　And dwells in glory by the throne of God.

Crowding across the deck, they seize the boats;
　　The mothers we revere are thrust away—
The wives we love repulsed—the girls adored
　　Are pushed apart—the child may vainly pray
With pleading tongue for succour. As bereft
　　Of noble feeling, and of manly pride,
They fill the boats, push off, and women left
　　To death, the cowards stem the heaving tide.

God! Can it be so? In an hour like this,
　　Can things in our clay shapen, thus forget
That woman bore and nursed them—that her blood
　　Runs pulsing through their arteries, even yet?
Are men like these our brethren? Are they framed
　　As we are? Have they hearts, or merely bone
And soulless reservoirs of life, that hold
　　No more of feelings than the insentient stone?

True to his duty yet, one mate remains
　　Beside her captain. Yet all toil is vain,

For terror will not pause, and sinking fast,
　　The laboring steamer settles in the main.
One chance is left. A raft is partly made—
　　Those who will hope may look for safety, here,
But blinded to their only means of flight,
　　Those left on board are swayed by hopeless fear.

They pour athwart the vessel's side. They throng
　　The boat and raft with desperation's heart—
Dorian, compelled to loose his fragile skiff,
　　Swings from the steamer, yet forbears to part
His chance from theirs. He bids his captain yet
　　Have heart. He will not leave them. Idle words.
The vessel's stern sinks slowly in the sea—
　　A single wild and maddening shriek is heard.

Another rises. It is woman's cry.
　　Appealing in that hour of dread to heaven.
Another and the steamer sinks. Their doom
　　Is registered. Accusing woman driven
To death by coward man, was heard by Him
　　Who holds the scales of justice. Mighty God!
We bow before Thee. In Thy will we own
　　Their fate. In tears we bend beneath the rod.

But Thou art just—with equal hand to weigh,
　　Our need of scourge, and those through whose weak will,
And selfish hearts, it smote us. As we taste
　　The bitter cup, Thy fingers fill, we feel
Thou wilt remember this. Thine outstretched arm
　　May pause, but slumbers not. We dare not pine,
For Thou hast willed it. But we trust Thy Word!
　　What is it? "Vengeance," saith the Lord, "is mine."

GLOSSARY

Aback: A sail is aback when the wind pushes it back against the mast or rigging in a direction opposite to that which was intended. Sails can be put aback deliberately, as in heaving to.

Abaft: Toward the stern; behind some specific point or object on a vessel.

Abeam: Ninety degrees from the centerline of a vessel. Also referred to as *broad on the beam* or *off the beam*.

Aft: Behind the midpoint of a vessel.

Aloft: Overhead, above.

Amidships: The center of a vessel relative to either length or breadth.

Back: When the wind shifts counterclockwise, it is said to back. When a ship is backed, she is positioned so that the wind pushes against the front of her sails and slows the vessel.

Ballast: Weight placed in the bottom of a vessel to add stability.

Bark: A three-masted vessel, having her fore and mainmasts rigged like a ship's, and her mizzenmast like the mainmast of a schooner, with no sail upon it but a spanker, and gaff-topsail.

Beam: The greatest width of a vessel.

Bearing: The direction from a ship to an object, such as another ship or a land feature, or to a compass point.

Berth: A bed aboard ship. Also, a term used to describe a vessel at a dock. She is said to be safe in her berth.

Bilge: The bottom of a vessel's hold nearest the keel.

Bitts: Perpendicular pieces of timber going up through the deck, placed to secure anything to.

Blanket: One sail blankets another when it blocks the wind from the other.

Bow: The front end of a vessel.

Bowsprit: A long spar jutting from the bow. A jibboom is attached to a bowsprit, adding to the overall length of the spar.

Brace: Lines used to pivot the yards supporting square-rigged sails.

Brails: Ropes by which the foot or lower corners of fore-and-aft sails are hauled up. To brail in, the act of hauling up such a sail.

Bulkhead: A vertical partition inside a cabin, similar to an interior wall in a house.

Bulwarks: The part of the sides of the ship that rises above the deck to create a wall-like structure.

Cable: A large, strong rope.

Claw off: To work a ship away from a lee shore.

Cutwater: The forward edge of the stem, or front piece of the bow, especially at the waterline.

Davits: Arms suspended over the side used to raise and lower a ship's boat, such as a lifeboat.

Dead reckoning: Deduction of a ship's position based on course, speed, and time, without recourse to celestial observations.

Deckhouse: A houselike structure built on deck, usually to house the crew and galley.

Draft: The depth of the keel below the surface of the water.

Ebb tide: When the tide flows away from shore out to sea.

Fiddles: Wooden barriers around the edge of a table or counter to help prevent objects from sliding off in heavy weather.

Flood tide: A tide flowing toward shore.

Footropes: Ropes suspended under the yards. Sailors stand on these as they work the sails.

Forecastle: The cabin in the bow of a vessel, typically used for crew's quarters. Pronounced fo'c's'l.

Foremast: The mast closest to the bow.

Forward: The direction from the midpoint of a vessel toward the bow.

Furl: To gather in a sail.

Gaff: A spar to which the head of a fore-and-aft sail is attached.

Halyard: A rope used to raise or lower a sail, or a spar.

Hatch: An opening in the deck that can be closed or opened.

Hawsehole: An opening in the hull at the bow through which the anchor chain or line passes.

Headsails: Sails set forward of the fore or mainmast.

Heave to: To adjust a sailing vessel's sails so as to greatly reduce forward motion. A ship might heave to in rough weather, or to speak another ship.

Jib: A triangular fore-and-aft sail set from the foremast and attached to the bowsprit and jibboom at the bow.

Jibboom: A spar attached to a ship's bowsprit.

Keel: The major longitudinal part of the hull, the backbone of a ship.

Knot: A term used to describe a vessel's speed through the water. It is equal to one nautical mile, or 6,080 feet.

Latitude: Lines drawn on a globe to measure distance north or south of the equator. The equator is marked as zero, and latitude measurements are designated in degrees north or south to the poles.

Lee: The side sheltered from the wind. A vessel can be in the lee of something, such as a land mass, that blocks the wind and waves.

Lee rail: The rail that is away from the direction from which the wind blows. When a ship heels, the lower side is the lee rail. The high side is the windward rail.

Lee shore: A shore to leeward of a vessel. Very dangerous for a sailing vessel because the wind may blow her ashore.

Leeward: Away from the direction the wind blows.

Leeway: The sideways motion a vessel makes when the wind, waves, or current pushes her off course.

List: The inclination of a vessel to one side, as a list to port or a list to starboard.

Log: A device used to measure a vessel's speed. *See also* Logbook.

Logbook: A document used to record daily course, wind direction, weather, and other details.

Longitude: Lines of measurement on the globe from pole to pole used to denote position east or west of the prime meridian at zero degrees, Greenwich, England.

Mainmast: The principal mast on a fore-and-aft rigged sailing vessel. It is set aft of the foremast on schooners.

Main topmast: A spar fixed to the mainmast. It extends the total length of the rig and allows a main gaff topsail to be set.

Masthead: The top portion of a mast.

Mizzenmast: The aft mast on a full-rigged ship.

Painter: A line attached to the bow of a ship's boat.

Pilot: A mariner specializing in guiding ships in and out of ports.

Pilot boat: Schooners used to sail pilots offshore to meet inbound ships.

Plot: A mark on a chart to denote position. To plot is to mark the chart.

Poop deck: The aft deck on a merchant vessel.

Port: The left side of a vessel when facing the bow.

Quarter: The sides of a vessel closest to the stern. There is a port quarter and a starboard quarter.

Ratline: A rope tied between shrouds. It is a form of ladder the sailors climb to get aloft.

Reef: A shoal. Also a reduction of sail area. Sails are reefed to reduce strain on a vessel in heavy weather.

Royal yard: The third perpendicular spar on the mast of a full-rigged ship.

Schooner: A two-masted, fore-and-aft rigged sailing vessel with the mainmast situated aft.

Scuppers: Holes in bulwarks through which water drains overboard.

Sextant: An optical device used to measure a celestial body's angle of elevation above the horizon, known as an altitude. One of the tools used to find a ship's latitude and longitude.

Shroud: Part of a sailing vessel's standing rigging. It is a rope run from the mast down to the side of a ship to help support the mast.

Slack water: The time between tides when tidal currents are at their weakest.

Sloop: A single-masted, fore-and-aft rigged sailing vessel with a mainsail and a jib.

Spanker: The after sail of a ship or a bark.

Spars: A catch-all term used to describe masts, booms, gaffs, and the like.

Spencer: A fore-and-aft sail set on a gaff with no boom.

Standing rigging: Ropes used to support the masts.

Starboard: The right side of a vessel when facing the bow.

Stay: A part of a sailing vessel's standing rigging. It is a rope run from the masthead behind and in front of the mast.

Stern: The aft end of a vessel.

Sternway: A vessel's motion backward through the water.

Tack: To turn a sailing vessel's bow through the wind to bring the wind from one side to the other.

Taffrail: The rail at the stern of a vessel.

Topsides: The hull between the waterline and the deck.

Transom: Planking across the stern.

Watches: A period of time when sailors are on duty, usually four hours on and four hours off. Also, the part of the crew on duty during a particular watch.

Waterline: The meeting point of the hull and the surface of the water.

Ways: Part of the structure supporting a vessel while she is built and launched.

Windward: Toward the direction from which the wind blows. The wind blows over the windward, or weather, rail of a ship. If a ship sails to windward, she must be close-hauled, with sails sheeted tight.

Yard: The spar perpendicular to the mast on which a squaresail is set.

BIBLIOGRAPHY

Abbott, John S. C. "Ocean Life." *Harper's New Monthly Magazine* 5 (June–November 1852).

Albion, Robert G. *Square-Riggers on Schedule*. Princeton, N.J.: Princeton University Press, 1938.

———. *The Rise of New York Port, 1815–1860*. New York: Scribner's, 1970 (1939).

Brinnin, John Malcolm. *The Sway of the Grand Saloon*. New York: Delacorte Press, 1971.

Brown, Alexander Crosby. *A. C. Brown Papers*. Newport News, Va.: The Mariners' Museum.

———. *Women and Children Last*. New York: G. P. Putnam's Sons, 1961.

Dana, Richard Henry, Jr. *The Seaman's Friend*. Boston: Thomas Groom & Co., 1851. (Reprinted in 1979 by Scholars' Facsimiles & Reprints, Delmar, New York.)

Derks, Scott, ed. *The Value of a Dollar: Prices and Incomes in the United States, 1860–1999*. Lakeville, Conn.: GreyHouse Publishing, 1999.

Hamilton, James A. *Reminiscences of James A. Hamilton: or, Men and Events, at Home and Abroad, During Three Quarters of a Century*. New York: Charles Scribner & Company, 1869.

Hunt, Freeman, ed. "Collins's Steamship Arctic." *Hunt's Merchants' Magazine and Commercial Review* 24 (January–June 1851).

Johnson, Allen, and Dumas Malone, eds. *Dictionary of American Biography*, Vol. 2. New York: Charles Scribner's Sons, 1929.

Lindsay, W. S. *History of Merchant Shipping and Ancient Commerce*. 4 vols. London: Sampson Low, Marston, Low, and Searle, 1874, 1876.

Lord, Walter. *A Night to Remember*. New York: Bantam, 1997.

McClellan, Elisabeth. *Historic Dress in America, 1800–1870.* Philadelphia: George W. Jacobs & Co., 1910.

"Men Who Have Made Yachting: George Steers." *Rudder* (February 1906).

Nott, Charles C. "A Footnote to the Loss of the Arctic." *American Neptune* 19 (April 1959): 128–132. (Nott's letter contributed by Alexander Crosby Brown.)

Seward, William H. *Speech for the Collins Steamers, in the Senate of the United States, April 27, 1852.* Washington, D.C.: Buell & Blanchard, Printers, 1852.

"The Shipbuilders of America: George Steers." *United States Nautical Magazine, and Naval Journal* (July 1857).

Stuart, Charles B. *Naval and Mail Steamers of the United States.* New York: Charles B. Norton, Irving House, 1853.

Tute, Warren. *Atlantic Conquest: The Men and Ships of the Golden Age of Steam.* Boston: Little, Brown, 1962.

Whitney, Ralph. "The Unlucky Collins Line." *American Heritage* 7 (February 1957): 48–53, 100–102.

Wilson, David Harris. *A History of England.* New York: Holt, Rinehart and Winston, 1967.

ACKNOWLEDGMENTS

NO WORK OF HISTORICAL NARRATIVE would be possible without the help of many people. My wife, Elizabeth, encouraged me from the start of this book and assisted me with some of the research. I am grateful to my agent, Jill Grinberg, who has always believed in me as an author and has helped me achieve my objectives over many years. The support of my editor, Stephen Morrow, and other important individuals at The Free Press and Simon & Schuster, is much appreciated.

I thank my friends at The Mariners' Museum, Newport News, Virginia, Lisa Flick from photography services, and Gregg Cina from the museum's library. Both of them were helpful in my efforts to research *Arctic* for background information and photographic images. The staff of the New York Public Library, Drew University, Rutgers University, and my local library also played an essential part in my research.

Finally, I must express my gratitude to Walter Lord, author of *A Night to Remember*, the classic historical narrative he wrote in 1955 about the sinking of *Titanic*. Also, many thanks to his secretary, Lillian Pacifico, for her help. They both showed a deep interest in this book and in me as an author, and offered encouragement during the writing process. Just as important, Mr. Lord allowed me to use an original watercolor of *Arctic* from his private collection for the book jacket, showing the liner as she slipped stern first beneath the waves on that cold, foggy day off Newfoundland in September 1854.

INDEX

ABOUT THE AUTHOR

A N EXPERT SAILOR, David W. Shaw brings decades of experience as a seaman to his work as an author. The author of *Inland Passage*, *Daring the Sea*, and *Flying Cloud*, Shaw writes extensively for yachting magazines. He has contributed articles to *Sail*, *Cruising World*, *Offshore*, and many other boating publications. He lives in New Jersey with his wife, Elizabeth, and sails in Maine.